FRANCIS BACON

BY
LORD MACAULAY.

**Fredonia Books
Amsterdam, The Netherlands**

Francis Bacon

by
Thomas Babington Macaulay

ISBN: 1-58963-903-0

Copyright © 2002 by Fredonia Books

Reprinted from the 1886 edition

Fredonia Books
Amsterdam, The Netherlands
http://www.fredoniabooks.com

All rights reserved, including the right to reproduce this book, or portions thereof, in any form.

In order to make original editions of historical works available to scholars at an economical price, this facsimile of the original edition of 1886 is reproduced from the best available copy and has been digitally enhanced to improve legibility, but the text remains unaltered to retain historical authenticity.

INTRODUCTION.

MACAULAY'S Essay on "Lord Bacon" was first published in "The Edinburgh Review" for July, 1837, and included criticisms of an edition, in sixteen volumes, of Bacon's Works, by Basil Montagu, that had appeared between the years 1825 and 1834. The title of the Essay is here altered because Francis Bacon became in his last years Lord Verulam and Viscount St. Alban's, but was no more Lord Bacon than William Cecil, Baron Burleigh, was Lord Cecil. We remember men by titles of the highest rank they reached. All the dukedoms in England could have lain only as dust on the name of William Shakespeare. Francis Bacon died Lord St. Albans, but he lives by the higher name that his own genius exalted.

The most serviceable introduction to Macaulay's Essay on Bacon will be, I think, the citation of another view of Bacon's character, which forms part of an old study of "Realistic Philosophy and its Age," by Professor Kuno Fischer, one of the best living writers on the history of philosophy. I quote from a translation by the late John Oxenford:—

INTRODUCTION.

"The manner in which Bacon displayed himself as a political character, his own especial acts in this capacity seem diametrically opposed to his scientific greatness. This opposition has often been pointed out and lamented. Bacon has even been set up as an example to show how widely distinct from each other are the scientific and moral tendencies of a man— to how high a degree of internal contradiction the variance between these two characters can be brought. Mr. Macaulay, especially, has of late pushed this contradiction to such an extreme point that it seems insoluble, and the character of Bacon appears inexplicable. Macaulay pleads against Montagu on the subject of Bacon's moral worth; and it is well so to compare the two biographers (of whom the second is the panegyrist), that one may serve as a corrective to the other. For our own part, we shall neither defend nor attack Bacon's character, but simply explain it, and hence we look here for that intrinsic harmony which belongs to every important character. Taking everything into consideration, we must confess that the contradiction between Bacon the philosopher and Bacon the political character does not appear to us so violent as it is represented by Macaulay. Neither was the one (to use the expression of Macaulay, who infelicitously cites a Baconian figure of speech)— neither was the one a 'soaring angel,' nor the other a 'creeping snake,' Neither on the one side is there pure light, nor on the other is there mere shade, but on both sides is a compound of both. . . .

"There is no elastic morality; and Bacon's moral nature was as elastic, as facile, as completely directed towards practical ends, and as compliant with circumstances, as his intellect. It quite accorded with the key-note of his individuality. Here is the perceptible harmony of his character, which has often escaped notice, or (as in the case of Mr. Macaulay) has been missed altogether. We see in Bacon's moral character, as compared with his intellect, not a distinct being, but only the shadow of his individuality, which grew larger as its substance increased in power and importance. . . . If we compare Bacon's moral disposition with his scientific character, we shall find between the two not a puzzling contradiction, but, on the contrary, a natural analogy; only, the very peculiarities that were injurious and perilous with respect to his practical life were advantageous to his scientific pursuits. As the elements of science and life are distinct from each other, the expressions of the scientific and the moral character must be likewise different, even where they both agree in their common source. To certain temptations the mind that seeks after truth is never exposed. Certain rewards are beyond the power of science to bestow, and for such rewards the scientific character cannot think of acting. . . . The element of science is in itself pure.

In science there are no such vices as selfishness and venality. To transplant a character from the moral into the scientific element, we must leave out all that will not admit of this operation—every merely moral phenomenon. . . . The science which Bacon proposed to himself was highly favoured by his moral constitution. With respect to the passions, he was in a position of natural and therefore happy neutrality. His mind, never misled, never dazzled, never abandoned to the sway of exclusive affections, never chained to objects of the heart, could, with all the deeper interest and with all the greater clearness, direct itself to a comprehensive whole. His cool heart supported his penetrating intellect. . . . In a word, Bacon's character was as practical, as cool, as supple as the science which he desired and prescribed for his age."

H. M.

FRANCIS BACON.

It is hardly necessary to say that Francis Bacon was the son of Sir Nicholas Bacon, who held the great seal of England during the first twenty years of the reign of Elizabeth. The fame of the father has been thrown into shade by that of the son. But Sir Nicholas was no ordinary man. He belonged to a set of men whom it is easier to describe collectively than separately, whose minds were formed by one system of discipline, who belonged to one rank in society, to one university, to one party, to one sect, to one administration, and who resembled each other so much in talents, in opinions, in habits, in fortunes, that one character, we had almost said one life, may, to a considerable extent, serve for them all.

They were the first generation of statesmen by profession that England produced. Before their time the division of labour had, in this respect, been very imperfect. Those who had directed public affairs had been, with few exceptions, warriors or priests; warriors whose rude courage was neither guided by science nor softened by humanity, priests whose learning and abilities were habitually devoted to the defence of tyranny and imposture. The Hotspurs, the Nevilles, the Cliffords, rough, illiterate, and unreflecting, brought to the council-board the fierce and imperious disposition which they had acquired amidst the tumult of predatory war, or in the gloomy repose of the garrisoned and moated castle. On the other side was the calm and subtle prelate, versed in all that was then considered as learning, trained in the schools to manage words, and in the confessional to manage hearts, seldom superstitious, but skilful in practising on the superstition of others, false, as it was natural that a man should be whose profession imposed on all who were not saints the necessity of being hypocrites, selfish, as it was natural that a man should be who could form no domestic ties and cherish no hope of legitimate posterity, more attached to his order than to his country, and guiding the politics of England with a constant sideglance at Rome.

But the increase of wealth, the progress of knowledge, and the reformation of religion, produced a great change. The nobles ceased to be military chieftains; the priests ceased to possess a monopoly of learning; and a new and remarkable species of politicians appeared.

These men came from neither of the classes which had, till then, almost exclusively furnished ministers of state. They were all laymen; yet they were all men of learning; and they were all men of peace. They were not members of the aristocracy. They inherited no titles, no large domains, no armies of retainers, no fortified castles. Yet they were not low men, such as those whom princes, jealous of the power of nobility, have sometimes raised from forges and cobblers' stalls to the highest situations. They were all gentlemen by birth. They had all received a liberal education. It is a remarkable fact that they were all members of the same university. The two great national seats of learning had even then acquired the characters which they still retain. In intellectual activity, and in readiness to admit improvements, the superiority was then, as it has ever since been, on the side of the less ancient and splendid institution. Cambridge had the honour of educating those celebrated Protestant Bishops whom Oxford had the honour of burning; and at Cambridge were formed the minds of all those statesmen to whom chiefly is to be attributed the secure establishment of the reformed religion in the north of Europe.

The statesmen of whom we speak passed their youth surrounded by the incessant din of theological controversy. Opinions were still in a state of chaotic anarchy, intermingling, separating, advancing, receding. Sometimes the stubborn bigotry of the Conservatives seemed likely to prevail. Then the impetuous onset of the Reformers for a moment carried all before it. Then again the resisting mass made a desperate stand, arrested the movement, and forced it slowly back. The vacillation which at that time appeared in English legislation, and which it has been the fashion to attribute to the caprice and to the power of one or two individuals, was truly a national vacillation. It was not only in the mind of Henry that the new theology obtained the ascendant one day, and that the lessons of the nurse and of the priest regained their influence on the morrow. It was not only in the House of Tudor that the husband was exasperated by the opposition of the wife, that the son dissented from the opinions of the father, that the brother persecuted the sister, that one sister persecuted another. The principles of Conservation and Reform carried on their warfare in every part of society, in every congregation, in every school of learning, round the hearth of every private family, in the recesses of every reflecting mind.

It was in the midst of this ferment that the minds of the persons whom we are describing were developed. They were born Reformers. They belonged by nature to that order of men who always form the front ranks of the great intellectual progress. They were, therefore, one and all, Protestants. In religious matters, however, though there is no reason to doubt that they were sincere, they were by no means zealous. None of them chose to run the smallest personal risk during the reign of Mary. None of them favoured the unhappy attempt of Northumberland in favour of his daughter-in-law. None of them shared in the desperate councils of Wyatt. They contrived to have business on the Continent; or, if they stayed in England, they heard mass and kept Lent with great decorum. When those dark and perilous years had gone by, and when the crown had descended to a new sovereign, they took the lead in the reformation of the Church. But they proceeded, not with the impetuosity of theologians, but with the calm determination of statesmen. They acted, not like men who considered the Romish worship as a system too offensive to God, and too destructive of souls, to be tolerated for an hour, but like men who regarded the points in dispute among Christians as in themselves unimportant, and who were not restrained by any scruple of conscience from professing, as they had before professed, the Catholic faith of Mary,. the Protestant faith of Edward, or any of the numerous intermediate combinations which the caprice of Henry and the servile policy of Cranmer had formed out of the doctrines of both the hostile parties. They took a deliberate view of the state of their own country and of the Continent: they satisfied themselves as to the leaning of the public mind; and they chose their side. They placed themselves at the head of the Protestants of Europe, and staked all their fame and fortunes on the success of their party.

It is needless to relate how dexterously, how resolutely, how gloriously they directed the politics of

England during the eventful years which followed, how they succeeded in uniting their friends and separating their enemies, how they humbled the pride of Philip, how they backed the unconquerable spirit of Coligni, how they rescued Holland from tyranny, how they founded the maritime greatness of their country, how they outwitted the artful politicians of Italy, and tamed the ferocious chieftains of Scotland. It is impossible to deny that they committed many acts which would justly bring on a statesman of our time censures of the most serious kind. But, when we consider the state of morality in their age, and the unscrupulous character of the adversaries against whom they had to contend, we are forced to admit that it is not without reason that their names are still held in veneration by their countrymen.

There were, doubtless, many diversities in their intellectual and moral character. But there was a strong family likeness. The constitution of their minds was remarkably sound. No particular faculty was preeminently developed; but manly health and vigour were equally diffused through the whole. They were men of letters. Their minds were by nature and by exercise well fashioned for speculative pursuits. It was by circumstances, rather than by any strong bias of inclination, that they were led to take a prominent part in active life. In active life, however, no men could be more perfectly free from the faults of mere theorists and pedants. No men observed more accurately the signs of the times. No men had a greater practical acquaintance with human nature. Their policy was generally characterised rather by vigilance, by moderation, and by firmness, than by invention or by the spirit of enterprise.

They spoke and wrote in a manner worthy of their excellent sense. Their eloquence was less copious and less ingenious, but far purer and more manly than that of the succeeding generation. It was the eloquence of men who had lived with the first translators of the Bible, and with the authors of the Book of Common Prayer. It was luminous, dignified, solid, and very slightly tainted with that affectation which deformed the style of the ablest men of the next age. If, as sometimes chanced, these politicians were under the necessity of taking a part in the theological controversies on which the dearest interests of kingdoms were then staked, they acquitted themselves as if their whole lives had been passed in the Schools and the Convocation.

There was something in the temper of these celebrated men which secured them against the proverbial inconstancy both of the court and of the multitude. No intrigue, no combination of rivals, could deprive them of the confidence of their Sovereign. No parliament attacked their influence. No mob coupled their names with any odious grievance. Their power ended only with their lives. In this respect, their fate presents a most remarkable contrast to that of the enterprising and brilliant politicians of the preceding and of the succeeding generation. Burleigh was minister during forty years. Sir Nicholas Bacon held the great seal more than twenty years. Sir Walter Mildmay was Chancellor of the Exchequer twenty-three years. Sir Thomas Smith was Secretary of State eighteen years; Sir Francis Walsingham about as long. They all died in office, and in the enjoyment of public respect and royal favour. Far different had been the fate of Wolsey, Cromwell, Norfolk, Somerset, and Northumberland. Far different also was the fate of Essex, of Raleigh, and of the still more illustrious man whose life we propose to consider.

The explanation of this circumstance is perhaps contained in the motto which Sir Nicholas Bacon inscribed over the entrance of his hall at Gorhambury, *Mediocria firma*. This maxim was constantly borne in mind by himself and his colleagues. They were more solicitous to lay the foundations of their power deep than to raise the structure to a conspicuous but insecure height. None of them aspired to be sole Minister. None of them provoked envy by an ostentatious display of wealth and influence. None of them affected to outshine the ancient aristocracy of the kingdom. They were free from that childish love of titles which characterised the successful courtiers of the generation which preceded them, and of that which followed them. Only one of those whom we have named was made a peer; and he was content with the lowest degree of the peerage. As to money, none of them could, in that age, justly be considered as rapacious. Some of them would, even in our time, deserve the praise of eminent disinterestedness. Their fidelity to the state was incorruptible. Their private morals were without stain. Their households were sober and well-governed.

Among these statesmen Sir Nicholas Bacon was generally considered as ranking next to Burleigh. He was called by Camden "Sacris conciliis alterum columen;" and by George Buchanan,

"Diu Britannici
Regni secundum columen."

The second wife of Sir Nicholas and mother of Francis Bacon was Anne, one of the daughters of Sir Anthony Cooke, a man of distinguished learning who had been tutor to Edward the Sixth. Sir Anthony had paid considerable attention to the education of his daughters, and lived to see them all splendidly and happily married. Their classical acquirements made them conspicuous even among the women of fashion of that age. Katherine, who became Lady Killigrew, wrote Latin Hexameters and Pentameters, which would appear with credit in the *Musæ Etonenses*. Mildred, the wife of Lord Burleigh, was described by

Roger Ascham as the best Greek scholar among the young women of England, Lady Jane Grey always excepted. Anne, the mother of Francis Bacon, was distinguished both as a linguist and as a theologian. She corresponded in Greek with Bishop Jewel, and translated his *Apologia* from the Latin so correctly, that neither he nor Archbishop Parker could suggest a single alteration. She also translated a series of sermons on fate and free-will from the Tuscan of Bernardo Ochino. This fact is the more curious, because Ochino was one of that small and audacious band of Italian reformers, anathematised alike by Wittenberg, by Geneva, by Zurich, and by Rome, from which the Socinian sect deduces its origin.

Lady Bacon was doubtless a lady of highly cultivated mind after the fashion of her age. But we must not suffer ourselves to be deluded into the belief that she and her sisters were more accomplished women than many who are now living. On this subject there is, we think, much misapprehension. We have often heard men who wish, as almost all men of sense wish, that women should be highly educated, speak with rapture of the English ladies of the sixteenth century, and lament that they can find no modern damsel resembling those fair pupils of Ascham and Aylmer who compared, over their embroidery, the styles of Isocrates and Lysias, and who, while the horns were sounding and the dogs in full cry, sat in the lonely oriel, with eyes riveted to that immortal page which tells how meekly and bravely the first great martyr of intellectual liberty took the cup from his weeping gaoler. But surely these complaints have very little foundation. We would by no means disparage the ladies of the sixteenth century or their pursuits. But we conceive that those who extol them at the expense of the women of our time forget one very obvious and very important circumstance. In the time of Henry the Eighth and Edward the Sixth, a person who did not read Greek and Latin could read nothing, or next to nothing. The Italian was the only modern language which possessed anything that could be called a literature. All the valuable books then extant in all the vernacular dialects of Europe would hardly have filled a single shelf. England did not yet possess Shakespeare's plays and the Fairy Queen, nor France Montaigne's Essays, nor Spain Don Quixote. In looking round a well-furnished library, how many English or French books can we find which were extant when Lady Jane Grey and Queen Elizabeth received their education? Chaucer, Gower, Froissart, Comines, Rabelais, nearly complete the list. It was therefore absolutely necessary that a woman should be uneducated or classically educated. Indeed, without a knowledge of one of the ancient languages no person could then have any clear notion of what was passing in the political, the literary, or the religious world.

The Latin was in the sixteenth century all, and more than all, that the French was in the eighteenth. It was the language of courts as well as of the schools. It was the language of diplomacy; it was the language of theological and political controversy. Being a fixed language, while the living languages were in a state of fluctuation, and being universally known to the learned and the polite, it was employed by almost every writer who aspired to a wide and durable reputation. A person who was ignorant of it was shut out from all acquaintance, not merely with Cicero and Virgil, not merely with heavy treatises on canon-law and school-divinity, but with the most interesting memoirs, state papers, and pamphlets of his own time, nay, even with the most admired poetry and the most popular squibs which appeared on the fleeting topics of the day, with Buchanan's complimentary verses, with Erasmus's dialogues, with Hutten's epistles.

This is no longer the case. All political and religious controversy is now conducted in the modern languages. The ancient tongues are used only in comments on the ancient writers. The great productions of Athenian and Roman genius are indeed still what they were. But though their positive value is unchanged, their relative value, when compared with the whole mass of mental wealth possessed by mankind, has been constantly falling. They were the intellectual all of our ancestors. They are but a part of our treasures. Over what tragedy could Lady Jane Grey have wept, over what comedy could she have smiled, if the ancient dramatists had not been in her library? A modern reader can make shift without Œdipus and Medea, while he possesses Othello and Hamlet. If he knows nothing of Pyrgopolynices and Thraso, he is familiar with Bobadil, and Bessus, and Pistol, and Parolles. If he cannot enjoy the delicious irony of Plato, he may find some compensation in that of Pascal. If he is shut out from Nephelococcygia, he may take refuge in Lilliput. We are guilty, we hope, of no irreverence towards those great nations to which the human race owes art, science, taste, civil and intellectual freedom, when we say that the stock bequeathed by them to us has been so carefully improved that the accumulated interest now exceeds the principal. We believe that the books which have been written in the languages of western Europe during the last two hundred and fifty years—translations from the ancient languages of course included—are of greater value than all the books which at the beginning of that period were extant in the world. With the modern languages of Europe English women are at least as well acquainted as English men. When, therefore, we compare the acquirements of Lady Jane Grey with those of an accomplished young woman of our own time, we have no hesitation in awarding the superiority to the latter. We hope that our readers will pardon this digression. It is long; but it can hardly be called unseasonable, if it tends to convince them that they are mistaken in thinking that the great-great-grandmothers of their great-great-grandmothers were superior women to their sisters and their wives.

Francis Bacon, the youngest son of Sir Nicholas, was born at York House, his father's residence in the Strand, on the twenty-second of January, 1561. The health of Francis was very delicate; and to this circumstance may be partly attributed that gravity of carriage, and that love of sedentary pursuits, which distinguished him from other boys. Everybody knows how much his premature readiness of wit and sobriety of deportment amused the Queen, and how she used to call him her young Lord Keeper. We are told that, while still a mere child, he stole away from his playfellows to a vault in St. James's Fields, for the purpose of investigating the cause of a singular echo which he had observed there. It is certain that, at only twelve, he busied himself with very ingenious speculations on the art of legerdemain; a subject which, as Professor Dugald Stewart has most justly observed, merits much more attention from philosophers than it has ever received. These are trifles. But the eminence which Bacon afterwards attained makes them interesting.

In the thirteenth year of his age he was entered at

Trinity College, Cambridge. That celebrated school of learning enjoyed the peculiar favour of the Lord Treasurer and the Lord Keeper, and acknowledged the advantages which it derived from their patronage in a public letter which bears date just a month after the admission of Francis Bacon. The master was Whitgift, afterwards Archbishop of Canterbury, a narrow-minded, mean, and tyrannical priest, who gained power by servility and adulation, and employed it in persecuting both those who agreed with Calvin about Church Government, and those who differed from Calvin touching the doctrine of Reprobation. He was now in a chrysalis state, putting off the worm and putting on the dragon-fly, a kind of intermediate grub between sycophant and oppressor. He was indemnifying himself for the court which he found it expedient to pay to the Ministers by exercising much petty tyranny within his own college. It would be unjust, however, to deny him the praise of having rendered about this time one important service to letters. He stood up manfully against those who wished to make Trinity College a mere appendage to Westminster School; and by this act, the only good act, as far as we remember, of his long public life, he saved the noblest place of education in England from the degrading fate of King's College and New College.

It has often been said that Bacon, while still at college, planned that great intellectual revolution with which his name is inseparably connected. The evidence on this subject, however, is hardly sufficient to prove what is in itself so improbable as that any definite scheme of that kind should have been so early formed, even by so powerful and active a mind. But it is certain that, after a residence of three years at Cambridge, Bacon departed, carrying with him a profound contempt for the course of study pursued there, a fixed conviction that the system of academic education in England was radically vicious, a just scorn for the trifles on which the followers of Aristotle had wasted their powers, and no great reverence for Aristotle himself.

In his sixteenth year he visited Paris, and resided there for some time, under the care of Sir Amias Paulet, Elizabeth's minister at the French court, and one of the ablest and most upright of the many valuable servants whom she employed. France was at that time in a deplorable state of agitation. The Huguenots and the Catholics were mustering all their force for the fiercest and most protracted of their many struggles; while the prince, whose duty it was to protect and to restrain both, had by his vices and follies degraded himself so deeply that he had no authority over either. Bacon, however, made a tour through several provinces, and appears to have passed some time at Poitiers. We have abundant proof that during his stay on the Continent he did not neglect literary and scientific pursuits. But his attention seems to have been chiefly directed to statistics and diplomacy. It was at this time that he wrote those Notes on the State of Europe which are printed in his works. He studied the principles of the art of deciphering with great interest, and invented one cipher so ingenious that, many years later, he thought it deserving of a place in the *De Augmentis*. In February, 1580, while engaged in these pursuits, he received intelligence of the almost sudden death of his father, and instantly returned to England.

His prospects were greatly overcast by this event. He was most desirous to obtain a provision which might enable him to devote himself to literature and politics. He applied to the Government; and it seems strange that he should have applied in vain. His wishes were moderate. His hereditary claims on the administration were great. He had himself been favourably noticed by the Queen. His uncle was Prime Minister. His own talents were such as any minister might have been eager to enlist in the public service. But his solicitations were unsuccessful. The truth is that the Cecils disliked him, and did all that they could decently do to keep him down. It has never been alleged that Bacon had done anything to merit this dislike; nor is it at all probable that a man whose temper was naturally mild, whose manners were courteous, who, through life, nursed his fortunes with the utmost care, and who was fearful even to a fault of offending the powerful, would have given any just cause of displeasure to a kinsman who had the means of rendering him essential service and of doing him irreparable injury. The real explanation, we believe, is this. Robert Cecil, the Treasurer's second son, was younger by a few months than Bacon. He had been educated with the utmost care, had been initiated, while still a boy, in the mysteries of diplomacy and court intrigue, and was just at this time about to be produced on the stage of public life. The wish nearest to Burleigh's heart was that his own greatness might descend to this favourite child. But even Burleigh's fatherly partiality could hardly prevent him from perceiving that Robert, with all his abilities and acquirements, was no match for his cousin Francis. This seems to us the only rational explanation of the Treasurer's conduct. Mr. Montagu is more charitable. He supposes that Burleigh was influenced merely by affection for his nephew, and was "little disposed to encourage him to rely on others rather than on himself, and to venture on the quicksands of politics, instead of the certain profession of the law." If such were Burleigh's feelings, it seems strange that he should have suffered his son to venture on those quicksands from which he so carefully preserved his nephew. But the truth is that, if Burleigh had been so disposed, he might easily have secured to Bacon a comfortable provision which should have been exposed to no risk. And it is certain that he showed as little disposition to enable his nephew to live by a profession as to enable him to live without a profession. That Bacon himself attributed the conduct of his relatives to jealousy of his superior talents, we have not the smallest doubt. In a letter written many years later to Villiers he expresses himself thus: "Countenance, encourage, and advance able men in all kinds, degrees, and professions. For in the time of the Cecils, the father and the son, able men were by design and of purpose suppressed."

Whatever Burleigh's motives might be, his purpose was unalterable. The supplications which Francis addressed to his uncle and aunt were earnest, humble, and almost servile. He was the most promising and accomplished young man of his time. His father had been the brother-in-law, the most useful colleague, the nearest friend of the Minister. But all this availed poor Francis nothing. He was forced, much against his will, to betake himself to the study of the law. He was admitted at Gray's Inn; and, during some years, he laboured there in obscurity.

What the extent of his legal attainments may have been it is difficult to say. It was not hard for a man of his powers to acquire that very moderate portion of technical knowledge which, when joined to quickness, tact, wit, ingenuity, eloquence, and knowledge of the world, is sufficient to raise an advocate to the highest professional eminence. The general opinion appears to have been that which was on one occasion expressed by Elizabeth. "Bacon," said she, "hath a great wit and much learning; but in law showeth to the uttermost of his knowledge, and is not deep." The Cecils, we suspect, did their best to spread this opinion by whispers and insinuations. Coke openly proclaimed it with that rancorous insolence which was habitual to him. No reports are more readily believed than those which disparage genius, and soothe the envy of conscious mediocrity. It must have been inexpressibly consoling to a stupid serjeant, the forerunner of him who, a hundred and fifty years later, "shook his head at Murray as a wit," to know that the most profound thinker and the most accomplished orator of the age was very imperfectly acquainted with the law touching *bastard eigné* and *mulier puisné*, and confounded the right of free fishery with that of common of piscary.

It is certain that no man in that age, or, indeed, during the century and a half which followed, was better acquainted than Bacon with the philosophy of law. His technical knowledge was quite sufficient, with the help of his admirable talents and of his insinuating address, to procure clients. He rose very rapidly into business, and soon entertained hopes of being called within the bar. He applied to Lord Burleigh for that purpose, but received a testy refusal. Of the grounds of that refusal we can, in some measure, judge by Bacon's answer, which is still extant. It seems that the old Lord, whose temper age and gout had by no means altered for the better, and who loved to mark his dislike of the showy, quick-witted young men of the rising generation, took this opportunity to read Francis a very sharp lecture on his vanity and want of respect for his betters. Francis returned a most submissive reply, thanked the Treasurer for the admonition, and promised to profit by it. Strangers, meanwhile, were less unjust to the young barrister than his nearest kinsman had been. In his twenty-sixth year he became a bencher of his Inn; and two years later he was appointed Lent reader. At length, in 1590, he obtained for the first time some show of favour from the Court. He was sworn in Queen's Counsel extraordinary. But this mark of honour was not accompanied by any pecuniary emolument. He continued, therefore, to solicit his powerful relatives for some provision which might enable him to live without drudging at his profession. He bore, with a patience and serenity which, we fear, bordered on meanness, the morose humours of his uncle, and the sneering reflections which his cousin cast on speculative men, lost in philosophical dreams, and too wise to be capable of transacting public business. At length the Cecils were generous enough to procure for him the reversion of the Registrarship of the Star Chamber. This was a lucrative place; but, as many years elapsed before it fell in, he was still under the necessity of labouring for his daily bread.

In the Parliament which was called in 1593 he sat as member for the county of Middlesex, and soon attained eminence as a debater. It is easy to perceive from the scanty remains of his oratory that the same compactness of expression and richness of fancy which appear in his writings characterised his speeches; and that his extensive acquaintance with literature and history enabled him to entertain his audience with a vast variety of illustrations and allusions, which were generally happy and apposite, but which were probably not least pleasing to the taste of that age when they were such as would now be thought childish or pedantic. It is evident also that he was, as indeed might have been expected, perfectly free from those faults which are generally found in an advocate who, after having risen to eminence at the bar, enters the House of Commons; that it was his habit to deal with every great question, not in small detached portions, but as a whole; that he refined little, and that his reasonings were those of a capacious rather than a subtle mind. Ben Jonson, a most unexceptionable judge, has described Bacon's eloquence in words, which, though often quoted, will bear to be quoted again. "There happened in my time one noble speaker who was full of gravity in his speaking. His language, where he could spare or pass by a jest, was nobly censorious. No man ever spoke more neatly, more pressly, more weightily, or suffered less emptiness, less idleness, in what he uttered. No member of his speech but consisted of his own graces. His hearers could not cough or look aside from him without loss. He commanded where he spoke, and had his judges angry and pleased at his devotion. No man had their affections more in his power. The fear of every man that heard him was lest he should make an end." From the mention which is made of judges, it would seem that Jonson had heard Bacon only at the Bar. Indeed, we imagine that the House of Commons was then almost inaccessible to strangers. It is not probable that a man of Bacon's nice observation would speak in Parliament exactly as he spoke in the Court of Queen's Bench. But the graces of manner and language must, to a great extent, have been common between the Queen's Counsel and the Knight of the Shire.

Bacon tried to play a very difficult game in politics. He wished to be at once a favourite at Court and popular with the multitude. If any man could have succeeded in this attempt, a man of talents so rare, of judgment so prematurely ripe, of temper so calm, and of manners so plausible, might have been expected to succeed. Nor, indeed, did he wholly fail. Once, however, he indulged in a burst of patriotism which cost him a long and bitter remorse, and which he never ventured to repeat. The Court asked for large subsidies and for speedy payment. The remains of Bacon's speech breathe all the spirit of the Long Parliament. "The gentlemen," said he, "must sell their plate, and the farmers their brass pots, ere this will be paid; and for us, we are here to search the wounds of the realm, and not to skim them over. The dangers are these. First, we shall breed discontent and endanger her Majesty's safety, which must consist more in the love of the people than their wealth. Secondly, this being granted in this sort, other princes hereafter will look for the like; so that we shall put an evil precedent on ourselves and our posterity; and in histories, it is to be observed, of all nations the English are not to be subject, base, or taxable." The Queen and her ministers resented this outbreak of public spirit in the highest manner. Indeed, many an honest member of the House of Commons had, for a much smaller matter, been sent to the Tower by the proud and hot-blooded Tudors. The young patriot condescended to make the most abject apologies. He adjured the Lord Treasurer to show some favour to his poor servant and ally. He bemoaned himself to the Lord Keeper, in a letter which may keep in countenance the most unmanly of the epistles which Cicero wrote during his banishment. The lesson was not thrown away. Bacon never offended in the same manner again.

He was now satisfied that he had little to hope from the patronage of those powerful kinsmen whom he had solicited during twelve years with such meek pertinacity; and he began to look towards a different quarter. Among the courtiers of Elizabeth had lately appeared a new favourite, young, noble, wealthy, accomplished, eloquent, brave, generous, aspiring; a favourite who had obtained from the grey-headed queen such marks of regard as she had scarce vouchsafed to Leicester in the season of the passions; who was at once the ornament of the palace and the idol of the city; who was the common patron of men of letters and of men of the sword; who was the common refuge of the persecuted Catholic and of the persecuted Puritan. The calm prudence which had enabled Burleigh to shape his course through so many dangers, and the vast experience which he had acquired in dealing with two generations of colleagues and rivals, seemed scarcely sufficient to support him in this new competition; and Robert Cecil sickened with fear and envy as he contemplated the rising fame and influence of Essex.

The history of the factions which, towards the close of the reign of Elizabeth, divided her court and her council, though pregnant with instruction, is by no means interesting or pleasing. Both parties employed the means which are familiar to unscrupulous statesmen; and neither had, or even pretended to have, any important end in view. The public mind was then reposing from one great effort, and collecting strength for another. That impetuous and appalling rush with which the human intellect had moved forward in the career of truth and liberty, during the fifty years which followed the separation of Luther from the communion of the Church of Rome, was now over. The boundary between Protestantism and Popery had been fixed very nearly where it still remains. England, Scotland, the Northern kingdoms were on one side; Ireland, Spain, Portugal, Italy, on the other. The line of demarcation ran, as it still runs, through the midst of the Netherlands, of Germany, and of Switzerland, dividing province from province, electorate from electorate, and canton from canton. France might be considered as a debatable land, in which the contest was still undecided. Since that time the two religions have done little more than maintain their ground. A few occasional incursions have been made. But the general frontier remains the same. During two hundred and fifty years no great society has risen up like one man, and emancipated itself by one mighty effort from the superstition of ages. This spectacle was common in the sixteenth century. Why has it ceased to be so? Why has so violent a movement been followed by so long a repose? The doctrines of the Reformers are not less agreeable to reason or to revelation now than formerly. The public mind is assuredly not less enlightened now than formerly. Why is it that Protestantism, after carrying everything before it in a time of comparatively little knowledge and little freedom, should make no perceptible progress in a reasoning and tolerant age; that the Luthers, the Calvins, the Knoxes, the Zwingles, should have left no successors; that during two centuries and a half fewer converts should have been brought over from the Church of Rome than at the time of the Reformation were sometimes gained in a year? This has always appeared to us one of the most curious and interesting problems in history. On some future occasion we may perhaps attempt to solve it. At present it is enough to say that, at the close of Elizabeth's reign, the Protestant party, to borrow the language of the Apocalypse, had left its first love and had ceased to do its first works.

The great struggle of the sixteenth century was over. The great struggle of the seventeenth century had not commenced. The confessors of Mary's reign were dead. The members of the Long Parliament were still in their cradles. The Papists had been deprived of all power in the state. The Puritans had not yet attained any formidable extent of power. True it is that a student, well acquainted with the history of the next generation, can easily discern in the proceedings of the last Parliaments of Elizabeth the germ of great and ever memorable events. But to the eye of a contemporary nothing of this appeared. The two sections of ambitious men who were struggling for power differed from each other on no important public question. Both belonged to the Established Church. Both professed boundless loyalty to the Queen. Both approved the war with Spain. There is not, as far as we are aware, any reason to believe that they entertained different views concerning the succession to the Crown. Certainly neither faction had any great measure of reform in view. Neither attempted to redress any public grievance. The most odious and pernicious grievance under which the nation then suffered was a source of profit to both, and was defended by both with equal zeal. Raleigh held a monopoly of cards, Essex a monopoly of sweet wines. In fact, the only ground of quarrel between the parties was that they could not agree as to their respective shares of power and patronage.

Nothing in the political conduct of Essex entitles him to esteem; and the pity with which we regard his early and terrible end is diminished by the consideration that he put to hazard the lives and fortunes of his most attached friends, and endeavoured to throw the whole country into confusion, for objects purely personal. Still, it is impossible not to be deeply interested for a man so brave, high-spirited, and generous; for a man who, while he conducted himself

towards his sovereign with a boldness such as was then
found in no other subject, conducted himself towards
his dependents with a delicacy such as has rarely been
found in any other patron. Unlike the vulgar herd of
benefactors, he desired to inspire, not gratitude, but
affection. He tried to make those whom he befriended
feel towards him as towards an equal. His mind,
ardent, susceptible, naturally disposed to admiration of
all that is great and beautiful, was fascinated by the
genius and the accomplishments of Bacon. A close
friendship was soon formed between them, a friendship
destined to have a dark, a mournful, a shameful end.

In 1594 the office of Attorney-General became vacant,
and Bacon hoped to obtain it. Essex made his friend's
cause his own, sued, expostulated, promised, threatened,
but all in vain. It is probable that the dislike felt by
the Cecils for Bacon had been increased by the connection which he had lately formed with the Earl.
Robert was then on the point of being made Secretary
of State. He happened one day to be in the same
coach with Essex, and a remarkable conversation took
place between them. "My Lord," said Sir Robert,
"the Queen has determined to appoint an Attorney-
General without more delay. I pray your Lordship
to let me know whom you will favour." "I wonder
at your question," replied the Earl. "You cannot but
know that resolutely, against all the world, I stand for
your cousin, Francis Bacon." "Good Lord!" cried

Cecil, unable to bridle his temper, "I wonder your Lordship should spend your strength on so unlikely a matter. Can you name one precedent of so raw a youth promoted to so great a place?" This objection came with a singularly bad grace from a man who, though younger than Bacon, was in daily expectation of being made Secretary of State. The blot was too obvious to be missed by Essex, who seldom forbore to speak his mind. "I have made no search," said he, "for precedents of young men who have filled the office of Attorney-General. But I could name to you, Sir Robert, a man younger than Francis, less learned, and equally inexperienced, who is suing and striving with all his might for an office of far greater weight." Sir Robert had nothing to say but that he thought his own abilities equal to the place which he hoped to obtain, and that his father's long services deserved such a mark of gratitude from the Queen; as if his abilities were comparable to his cousin's, or as if Sir Nicholas Bacon had done no service to the State. Cecil then hinted that, if Bacon would be satisfied with the Solicitorship, that might be of easier digestion to the Queen. "Digest me no digestions," said the generous and ardent Earl. "The Attorneyship for Francis is that I must have; and in that I will spend all my power, might, authority, and amity; and with tooth and nail procure the same for him against whomsoever; and whosoever getteth this office out of my hands for any other, before he have it, it shall cost him the coming by. And this be you assured of, Sir Robert, for now I fully declare myself; and for my own part, Sir Robert, I think strange both of my Lord Treasurer and you, that can have the mind to seek the preference of a stranger before so near a kinsman; for if you weigh in a balance the parts every way of his competitor and him, only excepting five poor years of admitting to a house of court before Francis, you shall find in all other respects whatsoever no comparison between them."

When the office of Attorney-General was filled up, the Earl pressed the Queen to make Bacon Solicitor-General, and, on this occasion, the old Lord Treasurer professed himself not unfavourable to his nephew's pretensions. But, after a contest which lasted more than a year and a half, and in which Essex, to use his own words, "spent all his power, might, authority, and amity," the place was given to another. Essex felt this disappointment keenly, but found consolation in the most munificent and delicate liberality. He presented Bacon with an estate worth near two thousand pounds, situated at Twickenham; and this, as Bacon owned many years after, "with so kind and noble circumstances as the manner was worth more than the matter."

It was soon after these events that Bacon first appeared before the public as a writer. Early in 1597 he published a small volume of Essays, which was afterwards enlarged by successive additions to many times its original bulk. This little work was, as it well deserved to be, exceedingly popular. It was reprinted in a few months; it was translated into Latin, French, and Italian; and it seems to have at once established the literary reputation of its author. But, though Bacon's reputation rose, his fortunes were still depressed. He was in great pecuniary difficulties; and, on one occasion, was arrested in the street at the suit of a goldsmith for a debt of three hundred pounds, and was carried to a spunging-house in Coleman Street.

The kindness of Essex was in the meantime indefatigable. In 1596 he sailed on his memorable expedition to the coast of Spain. At the very moment of his embarkation, he wrote to several of his friends, commending to them, during his own absence, the interests of Bacon. He returned, after performing the most brilliant military exploit that was achieved on the Continent by English arms during the long interval which elapsed between the battle of Agincourt and that of Blenheim. His valour, his talents, his humane and generous disposition, had made him the idol of his countrymen and had extorted praise from the enemies whom he had conquered. He had always been proud and headstrong, and his splendid success seems to have rendered his faults more offensive than ever. But to his friend Francis he was still the same. Bacon had some thoughts of making his fortune by marriage, and had begun to pay court to a widow of the name of Hatton. The eccentric manners and violent temper of this woman made her a disgrace and a torment to her connections. But Bacon was not aware of her faults, or was disposed to overlook them for the sake of her ample fortune. Essex pleaded his friend's cause with his usual ardour. The letters which the Earl addressed to Lady Hatton and to her mother are still extant, and are highly honourable to him. "If," he wrote, "she were my sister or my daughter, I protest I would as confidently resolve to further it as I now persuade you:" and again, "If my faith be anything, I protest, if I had one as near me as she is to you, I had rather match her with him, than with men of far greater titles." The suit, happily for Bacon, was unsuccessful. The lady, indeed, was kind to him in more ways than one. She rejected him; and she accepted his enemy. She married that narrow-minded, bad-hearted pedant, Sir Edward Coke, and did her best to make him as miserable as he deserved to be.

The fortunes of Essex had now reached their height, and began to decline. He possessed indeed all the qualities which raise men to greatness rapidly. But he had neither the virtues nor the vices which enable men to retain greatness long. His frankness, his keen sensibility to insult and injustice, were by no means agreeable to a sovereign naturally impatient of opposition, and accustomed, during forty years, to the most extravagant flattery, and the most abject submission. The daring and contemptuous manner in which he bade defiance to his enemies excited their deadly hatred. His administration in Ireland was unfortunate, and in many respects highly blamable. Though his brilliant courage and his impetuous activity fitted him admirably for such enterprises as that of Cadiz, he did not possess the caution, patience, and resolution necessary for the conduct of a protracted war, in which difficulties were to be gradually surmounted, in which much discomfort was to be endured, and in which few splendid exploits could be achieved. For the civil duties of his high place he was still less qualified. Though eloquent and accomplished, he was in no sense a statesman. The multitude indeed still continued to regard even his faults with fondness. But the Court had ceased to give him credit, even for the merit which he really possessed. The person on whom, during the decline of his influence, he chiefly depended, to whom he confided his perplexities, whose advice he solicited, whose intercession he employed, was his friend Bacon. The lamentable truth must be told. This friend, so loved, so trusted, bore a principal part in ruining the Earl's fortunes, in shedding his blood, and in blackening his memory.

But let us be just to Bacon. We believe that, to the

last, he had no wish to injure Essex. Nay, we believe
that he sincerely exerted himself to serve Essex, as
long as he thought that he could serve Essex without
injuring himself. The advice which he gave to his
noble benefactor was generally most judicious. He
did all in his power to dissuade the Earl from accepting the Government of Ireland. "For," says he, "I
did as plainly see his overthrow chained as it were by
destiny to that journey, as it is possible for a man to
ground a judgment upon future contingents." The
prediction was accomplished. Essex returned in disgrace. Bacon attempted to mediate between his friend
and the Queen; and, we believe, honestly employed all
his address for that purpose. But the task which he
had undertaken was too difficult, delicate, and perilous,
even for so wary and dexterous an agent. He had to
manage two spirits equally proud, resentful, and un-
governable. At Essex House he had to calm the rage
of a young hero incensed by multiplied wrongs and
humiliations, and then to pass to Whitehall for the purpose of soothing the peevishness of a sovereign, whose
temper, never very gentle, had been rendered morbidly
irritable by age, by declining health, and by the long
habit of listening to flattery and exacting implicit
obedience. It is hard to serve two masters. Situated
as Bacon was, it was scarcely possible for him to shape
his course so as not to give one or both of his employers
reason to complain. For a time he acted as fairly as,

in circumstances so embarrassing, could reasonably be expected. At length he found that, while he was trying to prop the fortunes of another, he was in danger of shaking his own. He had disobliged both the parties whom he wished to reconcile. Essex thought him wanting in zeal as a friend; Elizabeth thought him wanting in duty as a subject. The Earl looked on him as a spy of the Queen; the Queen as a creature of the Earl. The reconciliation which he had laboured to effect appeared utterly hopeless. A thousand signs, legible to eyes far less keen than his, announced that the fall of his patron was at hand. He shaped his course accordingly. When Essex was brought before the council to answer for his conduct in Ireland, Bacon, after a faint attempt to excuse himself from taking part against his friend, submitted himself to the Queen's pleasure, and appeared at the bar in support of the charges. But a darker scene was behind. The unhappy young nobleman, made reckless by despair, ventured on a rash and criminal enterprise, which rendered him liable to the highest penalties of the law. What course was Bacon to take? This was one of those conjunctures which show what men are. To a high-minded man, wealth, power, court-favour, even personal safety, would have appeared of no account, when opposed to friendship, gratitude, and honour. Such a man would have stood by the side of Essex at the trial, would have "spent all his power, might, authority, and amity" in soliciting a mitigation of the sentence, would have been a daily visitor at the cell, would have received the last injunctions and the last embrace on the scaffold, would have employed all the powers of his intellect to guard from insult the fame of his generous though erring friend. An ordinary man would neither have incurred the danger of succouring Essex, nor the disgrace of assailing him. Bacon did not even preserve neutrality. He appeared as counsel for the prosecution. In that situation, he did not confine himself to what would have been amply sufficient to procure a verdict. He employed all his wit, his rhetoric, and his learning, not to ensure a conviction—for the circumstances were such that a conviction was inevitable—but to deprive the unhappy prisoner of all those excuses which, though legally of no value, yet tended to diminish the moral guilt of the crime, and which, therefore, though they could not justify the peers in pronouncing an acquittal, might incline the Queen to grant a pardon. The Earl urged as a palliation of his frantic acts that he was surrounded by powerful and inveterate enemies, that they had ruined his fortunes, that they sought his life, and that their persecutions had driven him to despair. This was true; and Bacon well knew it to be true. But he affected to treat it as an idle pretence. He compared Essex to Pisistratus, who, by pretending to be in imminent danger of assassination, and by exhibiting self-inflicted wounds, succeeded in establishing tyranny at Athens. This was too much for the prisoner to bear. He interrupted his ungrateful friend by calling on him to quit the part of an advocate, to come forward as a witness, and to tell the Lords whether, in old times, he, Francis Bacon, had not, under his own hand, repeatedly asserted the truth of what he now represented as idle pretexts. It is painful to go on with this lamentable story. Bacon returned a shuffling answer to the Earl's question, and, as if the allusion to Pisistratus were not sufficiently offensive, made another allusion still more unjustifiable. He compared Essex to Henry Duke of Guise, and the rash attempt in the city to the day of the barricades at Paris. Why Bacon had recourse to such a topic it is difficult to say. It was quite unnecessary for the purpose of obtaining a verdict. It was certain to produce a strong impression on the mind of the haughty and jealous princess on whose pleasure the Earl's fate depended. The faintest allusion to the degrading tutelage in which the last Valois had been held by the House of Lorraine was sufficient to harden her heart against a man who in rank, in military reputation, in popularity among the citizens of the capital, bore some resemblance to the Captain of the League.

Essex was convicted. Bacon made no effort to save him, though the Queen's feelings were such that he might have pleaded his benefactor's cause, possibly with success, certainly without any serious danger to himself. The unhappy nobleman was executed. His fate excited strong, perhaps unreasonable feelings of compassion and indignation. The Queen was received by the citizens of London with gloomy looks and faint acclamations. She thought it expedient to publish a vindication of her late proceedings. The faithless friend who had assisted in taking the Earl's life was now employed to murder the Earl's fame. The Queen had seen some of Bacon's writings, and had been pleased with them. He was accordingly selected to write "A Declaration of the Practices and Treasons attempted and committed by Robert Earl of Essex," which was printed by authority. In the succeeding reign, Bacon had not a word to say in defence of this performance, a performance abounding in expressions which no generous enemy would have employed respecting a man who had so dearly expiated his offences. His only excuse was, that he wrote it by command, that he considered himself as a mere secretary, that he had particular instructions as to the way in which he was to treat every part of the subject, and that, in fact, he had furnished only the arrangement and the style.

We regret to say that the whole conduct of Bacon through the course of these transactions appears to Mr. Montagu not merely excusable, but deserving of high admiration. The integrity and benevolence of this gentleman are so well known that our readers will probably be at a loss to conceive by what steps he can have arrived at so extraordinary a conclusion; and we are half afraid that they will suspect us of practising some artifice upon them when we report the principal arguments which he employs.

In order to get rid of the charge of ingratitude, Mr. Montagu attempts to show that Bacon lay under greater obligations to the Queen than to Essex. What these obligations were it is not easy to discover. The situation of Queen's Counsel, and a remote reversion, were surely favours very far below Bacon's personal and hereditary claims. They were favours which had not cost the Queen a groat, nor had they put a groat into Bacon's purse. It was necessary to rest Elizabeth's claims to gratitude on some other ground; and this Mr. Montagu felt. "What perhaps was her greatest kindness," says he, "instead of having hastily advanced Bacon, she had, with a continuance of her friendship, made him bear the yoke in his youth. Such were his obligations to Elizabeth." Such indeed they were. Being the son of one of her oldest and most faithful ministers, being himself the ablest and most accomplished young man of his time, he had been condemned by her to drudgery, to obscurity, to poverty. She had depreciated his acquirements. She had checked him in the most imperious manner, when in Parliament he ventured to act an independent part. She had refused to him the professional advancement to which he had a just claim. To her it was owing that, while younger men, not superior to him in extraction, and far inferior to him in every kind of personal merit, were filling the highest offices of the state, adding manor to manor, rearing palace after palace, he was lying at a spunging-house for a debt of three hundred pounds. Assuredly if Bacon owed gratitude to Elizabeth, he owed none to Essex. If the Queen really was his best friend, the Earl was his worst enemy. We wonder that Mr. Montagu did not press this argument a little further. He might have maintained that Bacon was excusable in revenging himself on a man who had attempted to rescue his youth from the salutary yoke imposed on it by the Queen, who had wished to advance him hastily, who, not content with attempting to inflict the Attorney-Generalship upon him, had been so cruel as to present him with a landed estate.

Again, we can hardly think Mr. Montagu serious when he tells us that Bacon was bound for the sake of the public not to destroy his own hopes of advancement, and that he took part against Essex from a wish to obtain power which might enable him to be useful to his country. We really do not know how to refute such arguments except by stating them. Nothing is impossible which does not involve a contradiction. It is barely possible that Bacon's motives for acting as he did on this occasion may have been gratitude to the Queen for keeping him poor, and a desire to benefit his fellow-creatures in some high situation. And there is a possibility that Bonner may have been a good Protestant who, being convinced that the blood of martyrs is the seed of the Church, heroically went through all the drudgery and infamy of persecution, in order that he might inspire the English people with an intense and lasting hatred of Popery. There is a possibility that Jeffreys may have been an ardent lover of liberty, and that he may have beheaded Algernon Sydney, and burned Elizabeth Gaunt, only in order to produce a reaction which might lead to the limitation of the prerogative. There is a possibility that Thurtell may have killed Weare only in order to give the youth of England an impressive warning against gaming and bad company. There is a possibility that Fauntleroy may have forged powers of attorney, only in order that his fate might turn the attention of the public to the defects of the penal law. These things, we say, are possible. But they are so extravagantly improbable that a man who should act on such suppositions would be fit only for St. Luke's. And we do not see why suppositions on which no rational man would act in ordinary life should be admitted into history.

Mr. Montagu's notion that Bacon desired power only in order to do good to mankind appears somewhat strange to us, when we consider how Bacon afterwards used power, and how he lost it. Surely the service which he rendered to mankind by taking Lady Wharton's broad pieces and Sir John Kennedy's cabinet was not of such vast importance as to sanctify all the means which might conduce to that end. If the case were fairly stated, it would, we much fear, stand thus: Bacon was a servile advocate, that he might be a corrupt judge.

Mr. Montagu maintains that none but the ignorant and unreflecting can think Bacon censurable for anything that he did as counsel for the Crown, and that no advocate can justifiably use any discretion as to the party for whom he appears. We will not at present inquire whether the doctrine which is held on this subject by English lawyers be or be not agreeable to reason and morality; whether it be right that a man should, with a wig on his head, and a band round his neck, do for a guinea what, without those appendages, he would think it wicked and infamous to do for an empire; whether it be right that, not merely believing but knowing a statement to be true, he should do all that can be done by sophistry, by rhetoric, by solemn asseveration, by indignant exclamation, by gesture, by play of features, by terrifying one honest witness, by perplexing another, to cause a jury to think that statement false. It is not necessary on the present occasion to decide these questions. The professional rules, be they good or bad, are rules to which many wise and virtuous men have conformed, and are daily conforming. If, therefore, Bacon did no more than these rules required of him, we shall readily admit that he was blameless, or, at least, excusable. But we conceive that his conduct was not justifiable according to any professional rules that now exist, or that ever existed in England. It has always been held that, in criminal cases in which the prisoner was denied the help of counsel, and, above all, in capital cases, advocates were both entitled and bound to exercise a discretion. It is true, that, after the Revolution, when the Parliament began to make inquisition for the innocent blood which had been shed by the last Stuarts, a feeble attempt was made to defend the lawyers who had been accomplices in the murder of Sir Thomas Armstrong, on the ground that they had only acted professionally. The wretched sophism was silenced by the execrations of the House of Commons. "Things will never be well done," said Mr. Foley, "till some of that profession be made examples." "We have a new sort of monsters in the world," said the younger Hampden, "haranguing a man to death. These I call bloodhounds. Sawyer is very criminal and guilty of this murder." "I speak to discharge my conscience," said Mr. Galloway. "I will not have the blood of this man at my door. Sawyer demanded judgment against him and execution. I believe him guilty of the death of this man. Do what you will with him." "If the profession of the law," said the elder Hampden, "gives a man authority to murder at this rate, it is the interest of all men to rise and exterminate that profession."

Nor was this language held only by unlearned country gentlemen. Sir William Williams, one of the ablest and most unscrupulous lawyers of the age, took the same view of the case. He had not hesitated, he said, to take part in the prosecution of the bishops, because they were allowed counsel. But he maintained that, where the prisoner was not allowed counsel, the Counsel for the Crown was bound to exercise a discretion, and that every lawyer who neglected this distinction was a betrayer of the law. But it is unnecessary to cite authority. It is known to everybody who has ever looked into a court of quarter-sessions that lawyers do exercise a discretion in criminal cases; and it is plain to every man of common sense that, if they did not exercise such a discretion, they would be a more hateful body of men than those bravoes who used to hire out their stilettoes in Italy.

Bacon appeared against a man who was indeed guilty of a great offence, but who had been his benefactor and friend. He did more than this. Nay, he did more than a person who had never seen Essex would have been justified in doing. He employed all the art of an advocate in order to make the prisoner's conduct appear more inexcusable and more dangerous to the state than it really had been. All that professional duty could, in any case, have required of him, would have been to conduct the cause so as to ensure a conviction. But from the nature of the circumstances there could not be the smallest doubt that the Earl would be found guilty. The character of the crime was unequivocal. It had been committed recently, in broad daylight, in the streets of the capital, in the presence of thousands. If ever there was an occasion on which an advocate had no temptation to resort to extraneous topics, for the purpose of blinding the judgment and inflaming the passions of a tribunal, this was that occasion. Why then resort to arguments which, while they could add nothing to the strength of the case, considered in a legal point of view, tended to aggravate the moral guilt of the fatal enterprise, and to excite fear and resentment in that quarter from which alone the Earl could now expect mercy? Why remind the audience of the arts of the ancient tyrants? Why deny, what everybody knew to be the truth, that a powerful faction at court had long sought to effect the ruin of the prisoner? Why, above all, institute a parallel between the unhappy culprit and the most wicked and most successful rebel of the age? Was it absolutely impossible to do all that professional duty required without reminding a jealous sovereign of the League, of the barricades, and of all the humiliations which a too powerful subject had heaped on Henry the Third?

But if we admit the plea which Mr. Montagu urges in defence of what Bacon did as an advocate, what shall we say of the "Declaration of the Treasons of

Robert Earl of Essex?" Here, at least, there was no pretence of professional obligation. Even those who may think it the duty of a lawyer to hang, draw, and quarter his benefactors, for a proper consideration, will hardly say that it is his duty to write abusive pamphlets against them, after they are in their graves. Bacon excused himself by saying that he was not answerable for the matter of the book, and that he furnished only the language. But why did he endow such purposes with words? Could no hack writer, without virtue or shame, be found to exaggerate the errors, already so dearly expiated, of a gentle and noble spirit? Every age produces those links between the man and the baboon. Every age is fertile of Oldmixons, of Kenricks, and of Anthony Pasquins. But was it for Bacon so to prostitute his intellect? Could he not feel that, while he rounded and pointed some period dictated by the envy of Cecil, or gave a plausible form to some slander invented by the dastardly malignity of Cobham, he was not sinning merely against his friend's honour and his own? Could he not feel that letters, eloquence, philosophy, were all degraded in his degradation?

The real explanation of all this is perfectly obvious; and nothing but a partiality amounting to a ruling passion could cause anybody to miss it. The moral qualities of Bacon were not of a high order. We do not say that he was a bad man. He was not inhuman or tyrannical. He bore with meekness his high civil honours, and the far higher honours gained by his intellect. He was very seldom, if ever, provoked into treating any person with malignity and insolence. No man more readily held up the left cheek to those who had smitten the right. No man was more expert at the soft answer which turneth away wrath. He was never charged, by any accuser entitled to the smallest credit, with licentious habits. His even temper, his flowing courtesy, the general respectability of his demeanour, made a favourable impression on those who saw him in situations which do not severely try the principles. His faults were—we write it with pain— coldness of heart, and meanness of spirit. He seems to have been incapable of feeling strong affection, of facing great dangers, of making great sacrifices. His desires were set on things below. Wealth, precedence, titles, patronage, the mace, the seals, the coronet, large houses, fair gardens, rich manors, massy services of plate, gay hangings, curious cabinets, had as great attractions for him as for any of the courtiers who dropped on their knees in the dirt when Elizabeth passed by, and then hastened home to write to the King of Scots that her Grace seemed to be breaking fast. For these objects he had stooped to everything, and endured everything. For these he had sued in the humblest manner, and, when unjustly and ungraciously repulsed, had thanked those who had repulsed him, and had begun to sue again. For these objects, as soon as he found that the smallest show of independence in Parliament was offensive to the Queen, he had abased himself to the dust before her, and implored forgiveness in terms better suited to a convicted thief than to a knight of the shire. For these he joined, and for these he forsook, Lord Essex. He continued to plead his patron's cause with the Queen as long as he thought that by pleading that cause he might serve himself. Nay, he went further; for his feelings, though not warm, were kind; he pleaded that cause as long as he thought that he could plead it without injury to himself. But when it became evident that Essex was going headlong to his ruin, Bacon began to tremble for his own fortunes. What he had to fear would not indeed have been very alarming to a man of lofty character. It was not death. It was not imprisonment. It was the loss of court favour. It was the being left behind by others in the career of ambition. It was the having leisure to finish the *Instauratio Magna*. The Queen looked coldly on him. The courtiers began to consider him as a marked man. He determined to change his line of conduct, and to proceed in a new course with as much vigour as to make up for lost time. When once he had determined to act against his friend, knowing himself to be suspected, he acted with more zeal than would have been necessary or justifiable if he had been employed against a stranger. He exerted his professional talents to shed the Earl's blood, and his literary talents to blacken the Earl's memory.

It is certain that his conduct excited, at the time, great and general disapprobation. While Elizabeth lived, indeed, this disapprobation, though deeply felt, was not loudly expressed. But a great change was at hand. The health of the Queen had long been decaying; and the operation of age and disease was now assisted by acute mental suffering. The pitiable melancholy of her last days has generally been ascribed to her fond regret for Essex. But we are disposed to attribute her dejection partly to physical causes, and partly to the conduct of her courtiers and ministers. They did all in their power to conceal from her the intrigues which they were carrying on at the Court of Scotland. But her keen sagacity was not to be so deceived. She did not know the whole. But she knew that she was surrounded by men who were impatient for that new world which was to begin at her death, who had never been attached to her by affection, and who were now but very slightly attached to her by interest. Prostration and flattery could not conceal from her the cruel truth, that those whom she had trusted and promoted had never loved her, and were fast ceasing to fear her. Unable to avenge herself, and too proud to complain, she suffered sorrow and resentment to prey on her heart, till, after a long career of power, prosperity, and glory, she died sick and weary of the world.

James mounted the throne: and Bacon employed all his address to obtain for himself a share of the favour of his new master. This was no difficult task. The faults of James, both as a man and as a prince, were numerous; but insensibility to the claims of genius and learning was not among them. He was indeed made up of two men, a witty, well-read scholar, who wrote, disputed, and harangued, and a nervous, drivelling idiot, who acted. If he had been a Canon of Christ Church, or a Prebendary of Westminster, it is not improbable that he would have left a highly respectable name to posterity; that he would have distinguished himself among the translators of the Bible, and among the Divines who attended the Synod of Dort; and that he would have been regarded by the literary world as no contemptible rival of Vossius and Casaubon. But fortune placed him in a situation in which his weaknesses covered him with disgrace, and in which his accomplishments brought him no honour. In a college, much eccentricity and childishness would have been readily pardoned in so learned a man. But all that learning could do for him on the throne was to make people think him a pedant as well as a fool.

Bacon was favourably received at Court; and soon found that his chance of promotion was not diminished by the death of the Queen. He was solicitous to be knighted, for two reasons which are somewhat amusing. The King had already dubbed half London, and Bacon found himself the only untitled person in his mess at Gray's Inn. This was not very agreeable to him. He had also, to quote his own words, "found an Alderman's daughter, a handsome maiden, to his liking." On both these grounds, he begged his cousin, Robert Cecil, "if it might please his good Lordship," to use his interest in his behalf. The application was successful. Bacon was one of three hundred gentlemen who, on the coronation day, received the honour, if it is to be so called, of knighthood. The handsome maiden, a daughter of Alderman Barnham, soon after consented to become Sir Francis's lady.

The death of Elizabeth, though on the whole it improved Bacon's prospects, was, in one respect, an unfortunate event for him. The new King had always felt kindly towards Lord Essex, and, as soon as he came to the throne, began to show favour to the House of Devereux, and to those who had stood by that house in its adversity. Everybody was now at liberty to speak out respecting those lamentable events in which Bacon had borne so large a share. Elizabeth was scarcely cold, when the public feeling began to manifest itself by marks of respect towards Lord Southampton. That accomplished nobleman, who will be remembered to the latest ages as the generous and discerning patron of Shakespeare, was held in honour by his contemporaries chiefly on account of the devoted affection which he had borne to Essex. He had been tried and convicted together with his friend; but the Queen had spared his life, and, at the time of her death, he was still a prisoner. A crowd of visitors hastened to the Tower to congratulate him on his approaching deliverance. With that crowd Bacon could not venture to mingle. The multitude loudly condemned him; and his conscience told him that the multitude had but too much reason. He excused himself to Southampton by letter, in terms which, if he had, as Mr. Montagu conceives, done only what as a subject and an advocate he was bound to do, must be considered as shamefully servile. He owns his fear that his attendance would give offence, and that his professions of regard would obtain no credit. "Yet," says he, "it is as true as a thing that God knoweth, that this great change hath wrought in me no other change towards your Lordship than this, that I may safely be that to you now which I was truly before."

How Southampton received these apologies we are not informed. But it is certain that the general opinion was pronounced against Bacon in a manner not to be misunderstood. Soon after his marriage he put forth a defence of his conduct, in the form of a Letter to the Earl of Devon. This tract seems to us to prove only the exceeding badness of a cause for which such talents could do so little.

It is not probable that Bacon's Defence had much effect on his contemporaries. But the unfavourable impression which his conduct had made appears to have been gradually effaced. Indeed, it must be some very peculiar cause that can make a man like him long unpopular. His talents secured him from contempt, his temper and his manners from hatred. There is scarcely any story so black that it may not be got over by a man of great abilities, whose abilities are united with caution, good-humour, patience, and affability, who pays daily sacrifice to Nemesis, who is a delightful companion, a serviceable though not an ardent friend, and a dangerous yet a placable enemy. Waller, in the next generation, was an eminent instance of this. Indeed, Waller had much more than may at first sight appear in common with Bacon. To the higher intellectual qualities of the great English philosopher, to the genius which has made an immortal epoch in the history of science, Waller had indeed no pretensions. But the mind of Waller, as far as it extended, coincided with that of Bacon, and might, so to speak, have been cut out of that of Bacon. In the qualities which make a man an object of interest and veneration to posterity, they cannot be compared together. But in the qualities by which chiefly a man is known to his contemporaries, there was a striking similarity between them. Considered as men of the world, as courtiers, as politicians, as associates, as allies, as enemies, they had nearly the same merits and the same defects. They were not malignant. They were not tyrannical. But they wanted warmth of affection and elevation of sentiment. There were many things which they loved better than virtue, and which they feared more than guilt. Yet, even after they had stooped to acts of which it is impossible to read the account in the most partial narratives without strong disapprobation and contempt, the public still continued to regard them with a feeling not easily to be distinguished from esteem. The hyperbole of Juliet seemed to be verified with respect to them. "Upon their brows shame was ashamed to sit." Everybody seemed as desirous to throw a veil over their misconduct as if it had been his own. Clarendon, who felt, and who had reason to feel, strong personal dislike towards Waller, speaks of him thus: "There needs no more to be said to extol the excellence and power of his wit and pleasantness of his conversation, than that it was of magnitude enough to cover a world of very great faults, that is, so to cover them that they were not taken notice of to his reproach, viz., a narrowness in his nature to the lowest degree, an abjectness and want of courage to support him in any virtuous undertaking, an insinuation and servile flattery to the height the vainest and most imperious nature could be contented with. . . . It had power to reconcile him to those whom he had most offended and provoked, and continued to his age with that rare felicity, that his company was acceptable where his spirit was odious, and he was at least pitied where he was most detested." Much of this, with some softening, might, we fear, be applied to Bacon. The influence of Waller's talents, manners, and accomplishments, died with him; and the world has pronounced an unbiassed sentence on his character. A few flowing lines are not bribe sufficient to pervert the judgment of posterity. But the influence of Bacon is felt and will long be felt over the whole civilised world. Leniently as he was treated by his contemporaries, posterity has treated him more leniently still. Turn where we may, the trophies of that mighty intellect are full in view. We are judging Manlius in sight of the Capitol.

Under the reign of James, Bacon grew rapidly in fortune and favour. In 1604 he was appointed King's Counsel, with a fee of forty pounds a year; and a pension of sixty pounds a year was settled upon him. In 1607 he became Solicitor-General, in 1612 Attorney-General. He continued to distinguish himself in Parliament, particularly by his exertions in favour of one excellent measure on which the King's heart was set, the union of England and Scotland. It was not difficult for such an intellect to discover many irresistible arguments in favour of such a scheme. He conducted the great case of the *Post Nati* in the Exchequer Chamber; and the decision of the judges, a decision the legality of which may be questioned, but the beneficial effect of which must be acknowledged, was in a great measure attributed to his dexterous management. While actively engaged in the House of Commons and in the courts of law, he still found leisure for letters and philosophy. The noble treatise on the "Advancement of Learning," which at a later period was expanded into the *De Augmentis*, appeared in 1605. The "Wisdom of the Ancients," a work which, if it had proceeded from any other writer, would have been considered as a masterpiece of wit and learning, but which adds little to the fame of Bacon, was printed in 1609. In the meantime the *Novum Organum* was slowly proceeding. Several distinguished men of learning had been permitted to see sketches or detached portions of that extraordinary book; and, though they were not generally disposed to admit the soundness of the author's views, they spoke with the greatest admiration of his genius. Sir Thomas Bodley, the founder of one of the most magnificent of English libraries, was among those stubborn Conservatives who considered the hopes with which Bacon looked forward to the future destinies of the human race as utterly chimerical, and who regarded with distrust and aversion the innovating spirit of the new schismatics in philosophy. Yet even Bodley, after perusing the *Cogitati et Visa*, one of the most precious of those scattered leaves out of which the great oracular volume was afterwards made up, acknowledged that in "those very points, and in all proposals and plots in that book, Bacon showed himself a master-workman;" and that "it could not be gainsaid but all the treatise over did abound with choice conceits of the present state of learning, and with worthy contemplations of the means to procure it." In 1612 a new edition of the "Essays" appeared, with additions surpassing the original collection both in bulk and quality. Nor did these pursuits distract Bacon's attention from a work the most arduous, the most glorious, and the most useful that even his mighty powers could have achieved, "the reducing and re-compiling," to use his own phrase, "of the laws of England."

Unhappily, he was at that very time employed in perverting those laws to the vilest purposes of tyranny. When Oliver St. John was brought before the Star Chamber for maintaining that the King had no right to levy Benevolences, and was for his manly and constitutional conduct sentenced to imprisonment during the royal pleasure and to a fine of five thousand pounds, Bacon appeared as counsel for the prosecution. About the same time he was deeply engaged in a still more disgraceful transaction. An aged clergyman, of the name of Peacham, was accused of treason on account of some passages of a sermon which was found in his study. The sermon, whether written by him or not, had never been preached. It did not appear that he had any intention of preaching it. The most servile lawyers of those servile times were forced to admit that there were great difficulties both as to the facts and as to the law. Bacon was employed to remove those difficulties. He was employed to settle the question of law by tampering with the judges, and the question of fact by torturing the prisoner.

Three judges of the Court of King's Bench were tractable. But Coke was made of different stuff. Pedant, bigot, and brute as he was, he had qualities which bore a strong, though a very disagreeable, resemblance to some of the highest virtues which a public man can possess. He was an exception to a maxim which we believe to be generally true, that those who trample on the helpless are disposed to cringe to the powerful. He behaved with gross rudeness to his juniors at the bar, and with execrable cruelty to prisoners on trial for their lives. But he stood up manfully against the King and the King's favourites. No man of that age appeared to so little advantage when he was opposed to an inferior, and was in the wrong. But, on the other hand, it is but fair to admit that no man of that age made so creditable a figure when he was opposed to a superior, and happened to be in the right. On such occasions, his half-suppressed insolence and his impracticable obstinacy had a respectable and interesting appearance, when compared with the abject servility of the bar and of the bench. On the present occasion he was stubborn and surly. He declared that it was a new and highly improper practice in the judges to confer with a law-officer of the Crown about capital cases which they were afterwards to try; and for some time he resolutely kept aloof. But Bacon was equally artful and persevering. "I am not wholly out of hope," said he in a letter to the King, "that my Lord Coke himself, when I have in some dark manner put him in doubt that he shall be left alone, will not be singular." After some time Bacon's dexterity was successful; and Coke, sullenly and reluctantly, followed the example of his brethren. But in order to convict Peacham it was necessary to find facts as well as law. Accordingly, this wretched old man was put to the rack, and, while undergoing the horrible infliction, was examined by Bacon, but in vain. No confession could be wrung out of him; and Bacon wrote to the King, complaining that Peacham had a dumb devil. At length the trial came on. A conviction was obtained; but the charges were so obviously futile, that the government could not, for very shame, carry the sentence into execution; and Peacham was suffered to languish away the short remainder of his life in a prison.

All this frightful story Mr. Montagu relates fairly. He neither conceals nor distorts any material fact. But he can see nothing deserving of condemnation in

Bacon's conduct. He tells us most truly that we ought not to try the men of one age by the standard of another; that Sir Matthew Hale is not to be pronounced a bad man because he left a woman to be executed for witchcraft; that posterity will not be justified in censuring judges of our time, for selling offices in their courts, according to the established practice, bad as that practice was; and that Bacon is entitled to similar indulgence. "To persecute the lover of truth," says Mr. Montagu, "for opposing established customs, and to censure him in after ages for not having been more strenuous in opposition, are errors which will never cease until the pleasure of self-elevation from the depression of superiority is no more."

We have no dispute with Mr. Montagu about the general proposition. We assent to every word of it. But does it apply to the present case? Is it true that in the time of James the First it was the established practice for the law-officers of the Crown to hold private consultations with the judges, touching capital cases which those judges were afterwards to try? Certainly not. In the very page in which Mr. Montagu asserts that "the influencing a judge out of court seems at that period scarcely to have been considered as improper," he gives the very words of Sir Edward Coke on the subject. "I will not thus declare what may be my judgment by these auricular confessions of *new* and pernicious tendency, and *not according to the customs of the realm*." Is it possible to imagine that Coke, who had himself been Attorney-General during thirteen years, who had conducted a far greater number of important state-prosecutions than any other lawyer named in English history, and who had passed with scarcely any interval from the Attorney-Generalship to the first seat in the first criminal court in the realm, could have been startled at an invitation to confer with the Crown-lawyers, and could have pronounced the practice new, if it had really been an established usage? We well know that, where property only was at stake, it was then a common though a most culpable practice, in the judges, to listen to private solicitation. But the practice of tampering with judges in order to procure capital convictions we believe to have been new, first, because Coke, who understood those matters better than any man of his time, asserted it to be new; and secondly, because neither Bacon nor Mr. Montagu has shown a single precedent.

How then stands the case? Even thus: Bacon was not conforming to an usage then generally admitted to be proper. He was not even the last lingering adherent of an old abuse. It would have been sufficiently disgraceful to such a man to be in this last situation. Yet this last situation would have been honourable compared with that in which he stood. He was guilty of attempting to introduce into the courts of law an odious abuse for which no precedent could be found. Intellectually, he was better fitted than any man that England has ever produced for the work of improving her institutions. But, unhappily, we see that he did not scruple to exert his great powers for the purpose of introducing into those institutions new corruptions of the foulest kind.

The same, or nearly the same, may be said of the torturing of Peacham. If it be true that in the time of James the First the propriety of torturing prisoners was generally allowed, we should admit this as an excuse, though we should admit it less readily in the case of such a man as Bacon than in the case of an ordinary lawyer or politician. But the fact is, that the practice of torturing prisoners was then generally acknowledged by lawyers to be illegal, and was execrated by the public as barbarous. More than thirty years before Peacham's trial, that practice was so loudly condemned by the voice of the nation that Lord Burleigh found it necessary to publish an apology for having occasionally resorted to it. But, though the dangers which then threatened the government were of a very different kind from those which were to be apprehended from anything that Peacham could write, though the life of the Queen and the dearest interests of the state were in jeopardy, though the circumstances were such that all ordinary laws might seem to be superseded by that highest law, the public safety, the apology did not satisfy the country: and the Queen found it expedient to issue an order positively forbidding the torturing of state-prisoners on any pretence whatever. From that time, the practice of torturing, which had always been unpopular, which had always been illegal, had also been unusual. It is well known that in 1628, only fourteen years after the time when Bacon went to the Tower to listen to the yells of Peacham, the judges decided that Felton, a criminal who neither deserved nor was likely to obtain any extraordinary indulgence, could not lawfully be put to the question. We therefore say that Bacon stands in a very different situation from that in which Mr. Montagu tries to place him. Bacon was here distinctly behind his age. He was one of the last of the tools of power who persisted in a practice the most barbarous and the most absurd that has ever disgraced jurisprudence, in a practice of which, in the preceding generation, Elizabeth and her ministers had been ashamed, in a practice which, a few years later, no sycophant in all the Inns of Court had the heart or the forehead to defend.

Bacon far behind his age! Bacon far behind Sir Edward Coke! Bacon clinging to exploded abuses! Bacon withstanding the progress of improvement! Bacon struggling to push back the human mind! The words seem strange. They sound like a contradiction in terms. Yet the fact is even so: and the explanation may be readily found by any person who is not blinded by prejudice. Mr. Montagu cannot believe that so extraordinary a man as Bacon could be guilty of a bad action; as if history were not made up of the bad actions of extraordinary men, as if all the most noted destroyers and deceivers of our species, all the founders of arbitrary governments and false religions, had not been extraordinary men, as if nine-tenths of the calamities which have befallen the human race had any other origin than the union of high intelligence with low desires.

Bacon knew this well. He has told us that there are persons "*scientia tanquam angeli alati, cupiditatibus vero tanquam serpentes qui humi reptant;*" and it did not require his admirable sagacity and his extensive converse with mankind to make the discovery. Indeed, he had only to look within. The difference between the soaring angel and the creeping snake was but a type of the difference between Bacon the philosopher and Bacon the Attorney-General, Bacon seeking for truth, and Bacon seeking for the Seals. Those who survey only one half of his character may speak of him with unmixed admiration, or with unmixed contempt. But those only judge of him correctly who take in at one view Bacon in speculation and Bacon in action. They will have no difficulty in comprehending how one and the same man should have been far before his age and far behind it, in one line the boldest and most useful of innovators, in another line the most obstinate champion of the foulest abuses. In his library, all his rare powers were under the guidance of an honest ambition, of an enlarged philanthropy, of a sincere love of truth. There, no temptation drew him away from the right course. Thomas Aquinas could pay no fees. Duns Scotus could confer no peerages. The Master of the Sentences had no rich reversions in his gift. Far different was the situation of the great philosopher when he came forth from his study and his laboratory to mingle with the crowd which filled the galleries of Whitehall. In all that crowd there was no man equally qualified to render great and lasting services to mankind. But in all that crowd there was not a heart more set on things which no man ought to suffer to be necessary to his happiness, on things which can often be obtained only by the sacrifice of integrity and honour. To be the leader of the human race in the career of improvement, to found on the ruins of ancient intellectual dynasties a more prosperous and a more enduring empire, to be revered by the latest generations as the most illustrious among the benefactors of mankind, all this was within his reach. But all this availed him nothing while some quibbling special pleader was promoted before him to the bench, while some heavy country gentleman took precedence of him by virtue of a purchased coronet, while some pandar, happy in a fair wife, could obtain a more cordial salute from Buckingham, while some buffoon, versed in all the latest scandal of the court, could draw a louder laugh from James.

During a long course of years, Bacon's unworthy ambition was crowned with success. His sagacity early enabled him to perceive who was likely to become the most powerful man in the kingdom. He probably knew the King's mind before it was known to the King himself, and attached himself to Villiers, while the less discerning crowd of courtiers still continued to fawn on Somerset. The influence of the younger favourite became greater daily. The contest between the rivals might, however, have lasted long, but for that frightful crime which, in spite of all that could be effected by the research and ingenuity of historians, is still covered with so mysterious an obscurity. The descent of Somerset had been a gradual and almost imperceptible lapse. It now became a headlong fall; and Villiers, left without a competitor, rapidly rose to a height of power such as no subject since Wolsey had attained.

There were many points of resemblance between the two celebrated courtiers who, at different times, extended their patronage to Bacon. It is difficult to say whether Essex or Villiers was more eminently distinguished by those graces of person and manner which have always been rated in courts at much more than their real value. Both were constitutionally brave; and both, like most men who are constitutionally brave, were open and unreserved. Both were rash and headstrong. Both were destitute of the abilities and of the information which are necessary to statesmen. Yet both, trusting to the accomplishments which had made them conspicuous in tilt-yards and ball-rooms, aspired to rule the state. Both owed their elevation to the personal attachment of the sovereign; and in both cases this attachment was of so eccentric a kind that it perplexed observers, that it still continues to perplex historians, and that it gave rise to much scandal which we are inclined to think unfounded. Each of them treated the sovereign whose favour he enjoyed with a rudeness which approached to insolence. This petulance ruined Essex, who had to deal with a spirit naturally as proud as his own, and accustomed, during near half a century, to the most respectful observance. But there was a wide difference between the haughty daughter of Henry and her successor. James was timid from the cradle. His nerves, naturally weak, had not been fortified by reflection or by habit. His life, till he came to England, had been a series of mortifications and humiliations. With all his high notions of the origin and extent of his prerogatives, he was never his own master for a day. In spite of his kingly title, in spite of his despotic theories, he was to the last a slave at heart. Villiers treated him like one; and this course, though adopted, we believe, merely from temper, succeeded as well as if it had been a system of policy formed after mature deliberation.

In generosity, in sensibility, in capacity for friendship, Essex far surpassed Buckingham. Indeed, Buckingham can scarcely be said to have had any friend, with the exception of the two princes over whom successively he exercised so wonderful an influence. Essex was to the last adored by the people. Buckingham was always a most unpopular man, except perhaps for a very short time after his return from the childish visit to Spain. Essex fell a victim to the rigour of the government amidst the lamentations of the people. Buckingham, execrated by the people, and solemnly declared a public enemy by the representatives of the people, fell by the hand of one of the people, and was lamented by none but his master.

The way in which the two favourites acted towards Bacon was highly characteristic, and may serve to illustrate the old and true saying, that a man is generally more inclined to feel kindly towards one on whom he has conferred favours than towards one from whom he has received them. Essex loaded Bacon with benefits, and never thought that he had done enough. It seems never to have crossed the mind of the powerful and wealthy noble that the poor barrister whom he treated with such munificent kindness was not his equal. It was, we have no doubt, with perfect sincerity that the Earl declared that he would willingly give his sister or daughter in marriage to his friend. He was in general more than sufficiently sensible of his own merits; but he did not seem to know that he had ever deserved well of Bacon. On that cruel day when they saw each other for the last time at the bar of the Lords, Essex taxed his perfidious friend with unkindness and insincerity, but never with ingratitude. Even in such a moment, more bitter than the bitterness of death, that noble heart was too great to vent itself in such a reproach.

Villiers, on the other hand, owed much to Bacon. When their acquaintance began, Sir Francis was a man of mature age, of high station, and of established fame as a politician, an advocate, and a writer. Villiers was little more than a boy, a younger son of a house then of no great note. He was but just entering on the career of court favour; and none but the most discerning observers could as yet perceive that he was likely to distance all his competitors. The countenance and advice of a man so highly distinguished as the Attorney-General must have been an object of the highest importance to the young adventurer. But though Villiers was the obliged party, he was far less warmly attached to Bacon, and far less delicate in his conduct towards Bacon, than Essex had been.

To do the new favourite justice, he early exerted his influence in behalf of his illustrious friend. In 1616

Sir Francis was sworn of the Privy Council, and in March, 1617, on the retirement of Lord Brackley, was appointed Keeper of the Great Seal.

On the seventh of May, the first day of term, he rode in state to Westminster Hall, with the Lord Treasurer on his right hand, the Lord Privy Seal on his left, a long procession of students and ushers before him, and a crowd of peers, privy-councillors, and judges following in his train. Having entered his court, he addressed the splendid auditory in a grave and dignified speech, which proves how well he understood those judicial duties which he afterwards performed so ill. Even at that moment, the proudest moment of his life in the estimation of the vulgar, and, it may be, even in his own, he cast back a look of lingering affection towards those noble pursuits from which, as it seemed, he was about to be estranged. "The depth of the three long vacations," said he, "I would reserve in some measure free from business of estate, and for studies, arts, and sciences, to which of my own nature I am most inclined."

The years during which Bacon held the Great Seal were among the darkest and most shameful in English history. Everything at home and abroad was mismanaged. First came the execution of Raleigh, an act which, if done in a proper manner, might have been defensible, but which, under all the circumstances, must be considered as a dastardly murder. Worse was behind, the war of Bohemia, the successes of Tilly and Spinola, the Palatinate conquered, the King's son-in-law an exile, the house of Austria dominant on the Continent, the Protestant religion and the liberties of the Germanic body trodden under foot. Meanwhile, the wavering and cowardly policy of England furnished matter of ridicule to all the nations of Europe. The love of peace which James professed would, even when indulged to an impolitic excess, have been respectable, if it had proceeded from tenderness for his people. But the truth is that, while he had nothing to spare for the defence of the natural allies of England, he resorted without scruple to the most illegal and oppressive devices, for the purpose of enabling Buckingham and Buckingham's relations to outshine the ancient aristocracy of the realm. Benevolences were exacted. Patents of monopoly were multiplied. All the resources which could have been employed to replenish a beggared Exchequer, at the close of a ruinous war, were put in motion during this season of ignominious peace.

The vices of the administration must be chiefly ascribed to the weakness of the King and to the levity and violence of the favourite. But it is impossible to acquit the Lord Keeper of all share in the guilt. For those odious patents, in particular, which passed the Great Seal while it was in his charge, he must be held answerable. In the speech which he made on first taking his seat in his court, he had pledged himself to discharge this important part of his functions with the greatest caution and impartiality. He had declared that he " would walk in the light," " that men should see that no particular turn or end led him, but a general rule." Mr. Montagu would have us believe that Bacon acted up to these professions, and says that, "the power of the favourite did not deter the Lord Keeper from staying grants and patents when his public duty demanded this interposition." Does Mr. Montagu consider patents of monopoly as good things? Or does he mean to say that Bacon stayed every patent of monopoly that came before him? Of all patents in our history, the most disgraceful was that which was granted to Sir Giles Mompesson, supposed to be the original of Massinger's Overreach, and to Sir Francis Michell, from whom Justice Greedy is supposed to have been drawn, for the exclusive manufacturing of gold and silver lace. The effect of this monopoly was of course that the metal employed in the manufacture was adulterated to the great loss of the public. But this was a trifle. The patentees were armed with powers as great as have ever been given to farmers of the revenue in the worst governed countries. They were authorised to search houses and to arrest interlopers; and these formidable powers were used for purposes viler than even those for which they were given, for the wreaking of old grudges, and for the corrupting of female chastity. Was not this a case in which public duty demanded the interposition of the Lord Keeper? And did the Lord Keeper interpose? He did. He wrote to inform the King that he "had considered of the fitness and conveniency of the gold and silver thread business," "that it was convenient that it should be settled," that he "did conceive apparent likelihood that it would redound much to his Majesty's profit," that, therefore, "it were good it were settled with all convenient speed." The meaning of all this was, that certain of the house of Villiers were to go shares with Overreach and Greedy in the plunder of the public. This was the way in which, when the favourite pressed for patents, lucrative to his relations and to his creatures, ruinous and vexatious to the body of the people, the chief guardian of the laws interposed. Having assisted the patentees to obtain this monopoly, Bacon assisted them also in the steps which they took for the purpose of guarding it. He committed several people to close confinement for disobeying his tyrannical edict. It is needless to say more. Our readers are now able to judge whether, in the matter of patents, Bacon acted conformably to his professions, or deserved the praise which his biographer has bestowed on him.

In his judicial capacity his conduct was not less reprehensible. He suffered Buckingham to dictate many of his decisions. Bacon knew as well as any man that a judge who listens to private solicitations is a disgrace to his post. He had himself, before he was raised to the woolsack, represented this strongly to Villiers, then just entering on his career. "By no means," said Sir Francis, in a letter of advice addressed to the young courtier, "by no means be you persuaded to interpose yourself, either by word or letter, in any cause depending in any court of justice, nor suffer any great man to do it where you can hinder it. If it should prevail, it perverts justice; but, if the judge be so just and of such courage as he ought to be, as not to be inclined thereby, yet it always leaves a taint of suspicion behind it." Yet he had not been Lord Keeper a month when Buckingham began to interfere in Chancery suits; and Buckingham's interference was, as might have been expected, successful.

Mr. Montagu's reflections on the excellent passage which we have quoted above are exceedingly amusing. "No man," says he, "more deeply felt the evils which then existed of the interference of the Crown and of statesmen to influence judges. How beautifully did he admonish Buckingham, regardless as he proved of all admonition!" We should be glad to know how it can be expected that admonition will be regarded by him who receives it, when it is altogether neglected by him who gives it. We do not defend Buckingham: but what was his guilt to Bacon's? Buckingham was young, ignorant, thoughtless, dizzy with the rapidity of his ascent and the height of his position. That he should be eager to serve his relations, his flatterers, his mistresses, that he should not fully apprehend the immense importance of a pure administration of justice, that he should think more about those who were bound to him by private ties than about the public interest, all this was perfectly natural, and not altogether unpardonable. Those who entrust a petulant, hot-blooded, ill-informed lad with power, are more to blame than he for the mischief which he may do with it. How could it be expected of a lively page, raised by a wild freak of fortune to the first influence in the empire, that he should have bestowed any serious thought on the principles which ought to guide judicial decisions? Bacon was the ablest public man then living in Europe. He was near sixty years old. He had thought much, and to good purpose, on the general principles of law. He had for many years borne a part daily in the administration of justice. It was impossible that a man with a tithe of his sagacity and experience should not have known that a judge who suffers friends or patrons to dictate his decrees violates the plainest rules of duty. In fact, as we have seen, he knew this well: he expressed it admirably. Neither on this occasion nor on any other could his bad actions be attributed to any defect of the head. They sprang from quite a different cause.

A man who stooped to render such services to others

was not likely to be scrupulous as to the means by which he enriched himself. He and his dependents accepted large presents from persons who were engaged in Chancery suits. The amount of the plunder which he collected in this way it is impossible to estimate. There can be no doubt that he received very much more than was proved on his trial, though, it may be, less than was suspected by the public. His enemies stated his illicit gains at a hundred thousand pounds. But this was probably an exaggeration.

It was long before the day of reckoning arrived. During the interval between the second and third Parliaments of James, the nation was absolutely governed by the Crown. The prospects of the Lord Keeper were bright and serene. His great place rendered the splendour of his talents even more conspicuous, and gave an additional charm to the serenity of his temper, the courtesy of his manners, and the eloquence of his conversation. The pillaged suitor might mutter. The austere Puritan patriot might, in his retreat, grieve that one on whom God had bestowed without measure all the abilities which qualify men to take the lead in great reforms, should be found among the adherents of the worst abuses. But the murmurs of the suitor and the lamentations of the patriot had scarcely any avenue to the ears of the powerful. The King, and the minister who was the King's master, smiled on their illustrious flatterer. The whole crowd of courtiers and nobles sought his favour with emulous eagerness. Men of wit and learning hailed with delight the elevation of one who had so signally shown that a man of profound learning and of brilliant wit might understand, far better than any plodding dunce, the art of thriving in the world.

Once, and but once, this course of prosperity was for a moment interrupted. It should seem that even Bacon's brain was not strong enough to bear without some discomposure the inebriating effect of so much good fortune. For some time after his elevation, he showed himself a little wanting in that wariness and self-command to which, more than even to his transcendent talents, his elevation was to be ascribed. He was by no means a good hater. The temperature of his revenge, like that of his gratitude, was scarcely ever more than lukewarm. But there was one person whom he had long regarded with an animosity which, though studiously suppressed, was perhaps the stronger for the suppression. The insults and injuries which, when a young man struggling into note and professional practice, he had received from Sir Edward Coke, were such as might move the most placable nature to resentment. About the time at which Bacon received the Seals, Coke had, on account of his contumacious resistance to the royal pleasure, been deprived of his seat in the Court of King's Bench, and had ever since languished in retirement. But Coke's opposition to the Court, we fear, was the effect not of good principles, but of a bad temper. Perverse and testy as he was, he wanted true fortitude and dignity of character. His obstinacy, unsupported by virtuous motives, was not proof against disgrace. He solicited a reconciliation with the favourite, and his solicitations were successful. Sir John Villiers, the brother of Buckingham, was looking out for a rich wife. Coke had a large fortune and an unmarried daughter. A bargain was struck. But Lady Coke, the lady whom twenty years before Essex had wooed on behalf of Bacon, would not hear of the match. A violent and scandalous family quarrel followed. The mother carried the girl away by stealth. The father pursued them, and regained possession of his daughter by force. The King was then in Scotland, and Buckingham had attended him thither. Bacon was, during their absence, at the head of affairs in England. He felt towards Coke as much malevolence as it was in his nature to feel towards anybody. His wisdom had been laid to sleep by prosperity. In an evil hour he determined to interfere in the disputes which agitated his enemy's household. He declared for the wife, countenanced the Attorney-General in filing an information in the Star Chamber against the husband, and wrote letters to the King and the favourite against the proposed marriage. The strong language which he used in those letters shows that, sagacious as he was, he did not quite know his place, and that he was not fully acquainted with the extent either of Buckingham's power, or of the change which the possession of that power had produced in Buckingham's character. He soon had a lesson which he never forgot. The favourite received the news of the Lord Keeper's interference with feelings of the most violent resentment, and made the King even more angry than himself. Bacon's eyes were at once opened to his error, and to all its possible consequences. He had been elated, if not intoxicated, by greatness. The shock sobered him in an instant. He was all himself again. He apologised submissively for his interference. He directed the Attorney-General to stop the proceedings against Coke. He sent to tell Lady Coke that he could do nothing for her. He announced to both the families that he was desirous to promote the connection. Having given these proofs of contrition he ventured to present himself before Buckingham. But the young upstart did not think that he had yet sufficiently humbled an old man who had been his friend and his benefactor, who was the highest civil functionary in the realm, and the most eminent man of letters in the world. It is said that on two successive days Bacon repaired to Buckingham's house, that on two successive days he was suffered to remain in an antechamber among foot-boys, seated on an old wooden box, with the Great Seal of England at his side, and that when at length he was admitted, he flung himself on the floor, kissed the favourite's feet, and vowed never to rise till he was forgiven. Sir Anthony Weldon, on whose authority this story rests, is likely enough to have exaggerated the meanness of Bacon and the insolence of Buckingham. But it is difficult to imagine that so circumstantial a narrative, written by a person who avers that he was present on the occasion, can be wholly without foundation; and, unhappily, there is little in the character either of the favourite or of the Lord Keeper to make the narrative improbable. It is certain that a reconciliation took place on terms humiliating to Bacon, who never more ventured to cross any purpose of any body who bore the name of Villiers. He put a strong curb on those angry passions which had for the first time in his life mastered his prudence. He went through the forms of a reconciliation with Coke, and did his best, by seeking opportunities of paying little civilities, and by avoiding all that could produce collision, to tame the untameable ferocity of his old enemy.

In the main, however, Bacon's life, while he held the Great Seal, was, in outward appearance, most enviable. In London he lived with great dignity at York House, the venerable mansion of his father. Here it was that, in January, 1620, he celebrated his entrance into his sixtieth year amidst a splendid circle of friends. He had then exchanged the appellation of Keeper for the higher title of Chancellor. Ben Jonson was one of the party, and wrote on the occasion some of the happiest of his rugged rhymes. All things, he tells us, seemed to smile about the old house, " the fire, the wine, the men." The spectacle of the accomplished host, after a life marked by no great disaster, entering on a green old age, in the enjoyment of riches, power, high honours, undiminished mental activity, and vast literary reputation, made a strong impression on the poet, if we may judge from those well-known lines:—

"England's high Chancellor, the destined heir,
In his soft cradle, to his father's chair,
Whose even thread the Fates spin round and full
Out of their choicest and their whitest wool."

In the intervals of rest which Bacon's political and judicial functions afforded, he was in the habit of retiring to Gorhambury. At that place his business was literature, and his favourite amusement gardening, which in one of his most interesting Essays he calls " the purest of human pleasures." In his magnificent grounds he erected, at a cost of ten thousand pounds, a retreat to which he repaired when he wished to avoid all visitors, and to devote himself wholly to study. On such occasions, a few young men of distinguished talents were sometimes the companions of his retirement; and among them his quick eye soon discerned the superior abilities of Thomas Hobbes. It is not probable, however, that he fully appreciated the powers of his disciple, or foresaw the vast influence, both for good and for evil, which that most vigorous and acute of human intellects was destined to exercise on the two succeeding generations.

In January, 1621, Bacon had reached the zenith of his fortunes. He had just published the *Novum Organum;* and that extraordinary book had drawn forth the warmest expressions of admiration from the ablest men in Europe. He had obtained honours of a widely different kind, but perhaps not less valued by him. He had been created Baron Verulam. He had subsequently been raised to the higher dignity of Viscount St. Albans. His patent was drawn in the most flattering terms, and the Prince of Wales signed it as a witness. The ceremony of investiture was performed with great state at Theobalds, and Buckingham condescended to be one of the chief actors. Posterity has felt that the greatest of English philosophers could derive no accession of dignity from any title which James could bestow, and, in defiance of the royal letters patent, has obstinately refused to degrade Francis Bacon into Viscount St. Albans.

In a few weeks was signally brought to the test the value of those objects for which Bacon had sullied his integrity, had resigned his independence, had violated the most sacred obligations of friendship and gratitude, had flattered the worthless, had persecuted the innocent, had tampered with judges, had tortured prisoners, had plundered suitors, had wasted on paltry intrigues all the powers of the most exquisitely constructed intellect that has ever been bestowed on any of the children of men. A sudden and terrible reverse was at hand. A Parliament had been summoned. After six years of silence the voice of the nation was again to be heard. Only three days after the pageant which was performed at Theobalds in honour of Bacon, the Houses met.

Want of money had, as usual, induced the King to convoke his Parliament. It may be doubted, however, whether, if he or his ministers had been at all aware of the state of public feeling, they would not have tried any expedient, or borne with any inconvenience, rather than have ventured to face the deputies of a justly exasperated nation. But they did not discern those times. Indeed, almost all the political blunders of James, and of his more unfortunate son, arose from one great error. During the fifty years which preceded the Long Parliament, a great and progressive change was taking place in the public mind. The nature and extent of this change was not in the least understood by either of the first two Kings of the House of Stuart, or by any of their advisers. That the nation became more and more discontented every year, that every House of Commons was more unmanageable than that which had preceded it, were facts which it was impossible not to perceive. But the Court could not understand why these things were so. The Court could not see that the English people and the English Government, though they might once have been well suited to each other, were suited to each other no longer; that the nation had outgrown its old institutions, was every day more uneasy under them, was pressing against them, and would soon burst through them. The alarming phenomena, the existence of which no sycophant could deny, were ascribed to every cause except the true one. "In my first Parliament," said James, "I was a novice. In my next, there was a kind of beasts called undertakers," and so forth. In the third Parliament he could hardly be called a novice, and those beasts, the undertakers, did not exist. Yet his third Parliament gave him more trouble than either the first or the second.

The Parliament had no sooner met than the House of Commons proceeded, in a temperate and respectful, but most determined manner, to discuss the public grievances. Their first attacks were directed against those odious patents, under cover of which Buckingham and his creatures had pillaged and oppressed the nation. The vigour with which these proceedings were conducted spread dismay through the Court. Buckingham thought himself in danger, and, in his alarm, had recourse to an adviser, who had lately acquired considerable influence over him. Williams. Dean of

Westminster. This person had already been of great use to the favourite in a very delicate matter. Buckingham had set his heart on marrying Lady Catherine Manners, daughter and heiress of the Earl of Rutland. But the difficulties were great. The Earl was haughty and impracticable, and the young lady was a Catholic. Williams soothed the pride of the father, and found arguments which, for a time at least, quieted the conscience of the daughter. For these services he had been rewarded with considerable preferment in the Church; and he was now rapidly rising to the same place in the regard of Buckingham, which had formerly been occupied by Bacon.

Williams was one of those who are wiser for others than for themselves. His own public life was unfortunate, and was made unfortunate by his strange want of judgment and self-command at several important conjunctures. But the counsel which he gave on this occasion showed no want of worldly wisdom. He advised the favourite to abandon all thoughts of defending the monopolies, to find some foreign embassy for his brother Sir Edward, who was deeply implicated in the villainies of Mompesson, and to leave the other offenders to the justice of Parliament. Buckingham received this advice with the warmest expressions of gratitude, and declared that a load had been lifted from his heart. He then repaired with Williams to the royal presence. They found the King engaged in earnest consultation with Prince Charles. The plan of operations proposed by the Dean was fully discussed, and approved in all its parts.

The first victims whom the Court abandoned to the vengeance of the Commons were Sir Giles Mompesson and Sir Francis Michell. It was some time before Bacon began to entertain any apprehensions. His talents and his address gave him great influence in the house of which he had lately become a member, as indeed they must have done in any assembly. In the House of Commons he had many personal friends and many warm admirers. But at length, about six weeks after the meeting of Parliament, the storm burst.

A committee of the lower House had been appointed to inquire into the state of the Courts of Justice. On the fifteenth of March the chairman of that committee, Sir Robert Philips, member for Bath, reported that great abuses had been discovered. "The person," said he, "against whom these things are alleged is no less than the Lord Chancellor, a man so endued with all parts, both of nature and art, as that I will say no more of him, being not able to say enough." Sir Robert then proceeded to state, in the most temperate manner, the nature of the charges. A person of the name of Aubrey had a case depending in Chancery. He had been almost ruined by law expenses, and his patience had been exhausted by the delays of the court. He received a hint from some of the hangers-on of the

Chancellor that a present of one hundred pounds would expedite matters. The poor man had not the sum required. However, having found out an usurer who accommodated him with it at high interest, he carried it to York House. The Chancellor took the money, and his dependents assured the suitor that all would go right. Aubrey was, however, disappointed; for, after considerable delay, "a killing decree" was pronounced against him. Another suitor of the name of Egerton complained that he had been induced by two of the Chancellor's jackals to make his Lordship a present of four hundred pounds, and that, nevertheless, he had not been able to obtain a decree in his favour. The evidence to these facts was overwhelming. Bacon's friends could only entreat the House to suspend its judgment, and to send up the case to the Lords in a form less offensive than an impeachment.

On the nineteenth of March the King sent a message to the Commons, expressing his deep regret that so eminent a person as the Chancellor should be suspected of misconduct. His Majesty declared that he had no wish to screen the guilty from justice, and proposed to appoint a new kind of tribunal, consisting of eighteen commissioners, who might be chosen from among the members of the two Houses to investigate the matter. The Commons were not disposed to depart from their regular course of proceeding. On the same day they held a conference with the Lords.

and delivered in the heads of the accusation against
the Chancellor. At this conference Bacon was not
present. Overwhelmed with shame and remorse, and
abandoned by all those in whom he had weakly put
his trust, he had shut himself up in his chamber from
the eyes of men. The dejection of his mind soon dis-
ordered his body. Buckingham, who visited him by
the King's order, "found his Lordship very sick and
heavy." It appears from a pathetic letter which the
unhappy man addressed to the Peers on the day of the
conference, that he neither expected nor wished to sur-
vive his disgrace. During several days he remained in
his bed, refusing to see any human being. He passion-
ately told his attendants to leave him, to forget him,
never again to name his name, never to remember that
there had been such a man in the world. In the meantime, fresh instances of corruption were every day
brought to the knowledge of his accusers. The number
of charges rapidly increased from two to twenty-three.
The Lords entered on the investigation of the case with
laudable alacrity. Some witnesses were examined at
the bar of the House. A select committee was appointed to take the depositions of others; and the inquiry was rapidly proceeding, when, on the twenty-
sixth of March, the King adjourned the Parliament
for three weeks.

This measure revived Bacon's hopes. He made the
most of his short respite. He attempted to work on

the feeble mind of the King. He appealed to all the strongest feelings of James, to his fears, to his vanity, to his high notions of prerogative. Would the Solomon of the age commit so gross an error as to encourage the encroaching spirit of Parliaments? Would God's anointed, accountable to God alone, pay homage to the clamorous multitude? "Those," exclaimed Bacon, "who now strike at the Chancellor will soon strike at the Crown. I am the first sacrifice. I wish I may be the last." But all his eloquence and address were employed in vain. Indeed, whatever Mr. Montagu may say, we are firmly convinced that it was not in the King's power to save Bacon, without having recourse to measures which would have convulsed the realm. The Crown had not sufficient influence over the Parliament to procure an acquittal in so clear a case of guilt. And to dissolve a Parliament which is universally allowed to have been one of the best Parliaments that ever sat, which had acted liberally and respectfully towards the Sovereign, and which enjoyed in the highest degree the favour of the people, only in order to stop a grave, temperate, and constitutional inquiry into the personal integrity of the first judge in the kingdom, would have been a measure more scandalous and absurd than any of those which were the ruin of the House of Stuart. Such a measure, while it would have been as fatal to the Chancellor's honour as a conviction, would have endangered the very existence of the monarchy. The King, acting by the advice of Williams, very properly refused to engage in a dangerous struggle with his people, for the purpose of saving from legal condemnation a minister whom it was impossible to save from dishonour. He advised Bacon to plead guilty, and promised to do all in his power to mitigate the punishment. Mr. Montagu is exceedingly angry with James on this account. But, though we are, in general, very little inclined to admire that Prince's conduct, we really think that his advice was, under all the circumstances, the best advice that could have been given.

On the seventeenth of April the Houses reassembled, and the Lords resumed their inquiries into the abuses of the Court of Chancery. On the twenty-second, Bacon addressed to the Peers a letter, which the Prince of Wales condescended to deliver. In this artful and pathetic composition, the Chancellor acknowledged his guilt in guarded and general terms, and, while acknowledging, endeavoured to palliate it. This, however, was not thought sufficient by his judges. They required a more particular confession, and sent him a copy of the charges. On the thirtieth, he delivered a paper in which he admitted, with few and unimportant reservations, the truth of the accusations brought against him, and threw himself entirely on the mercy of his peers. "Upon advised consideration of the charges," said he, "descending into my own conscience, and calling my memory to account so far as I am able, I do plainly and ingenuously confess that I am guilty of corruption, and do renounce all defence."

The Lords came to a resolution that the Chancellor's confession appeared to be full and ingenuous, and sent a committee to inquire of him whether it was really subscribed by himself. The deputies, among whom was Southampton, the common friend, many years before, of Bacon and Essex, performed their duty with great delicacy. Indeed, the agonies of such a mind and the degradation of such a name might well have softened the most obdurate natures. "My Lords," said Bacon, "it is my act, my hand, my heart. I beseech your Lordships to be merciful to a broken reed." They withdrew; and he again retired to his chamber in the deepest dejection. The next day, the sergeant-at-arms and the usher of the House of Lords came to conduct him to Westminster Hall, where sentence was to be pronounced. But they found him so unwell that he could not leave his bed; and this excuse for his absence was readily accepted. In no quarter does there appear to have been the smallest desire to add to his humiliation.

The sentence was, however, severe, the more severe, no doubt, because the Lords knew that it would not be executed, and that they had an excellent opportunity of exhibiting, at small cost, the inflexibility of their justice, and their abhorrence of corruption. Bacon was condemned to pay a fine of forty thousand pounds, and to be imprisoned in the Tower during the King's pleasure. He was declared incapable of holding any office in the State or of sitting in Parliament; and he was banished for life from the verge of the court. In such misery and shame ended that long career of worldly wisdom and worldly prosperity.

Even at this pass Mr. Montagu does not desert his hero. He seems indeed to think that the attachment of an editor ought to be as devoted as that of Mr. Moore's lovers; and cannot conceive what biography was made for,

"If 'tis not the same
Through joy and through torment, through glory and shame."

He assures us that Bacon was innocent, that he had the means of making a perfectly satisfactory defence, that when he "plainly and ingenuously confessed that he was guilty of corruption," and when he afterwards solemnly affirmed that his confession was "his act, his hand, his heart," he was telling a great lie, and that he refrained from bringing forward proofs of his innocence because he durst not disobey the King and the favourite, who, for their own selfish objects, pressed him to plead guilty.

Now, in the first place, there is not the smallest reason to believe that, if James and Buckingham had thought that Bacon had a good defence, they would have prevented him from making it. What conceivable motive had they for doing so? Mr. Montagu perpetually repeats that it was their interest to sacrifice Bacon. But he overlooks an obvious distinction. It was their interest to sacrifice Bacon on the supposition of his guilt, but not on the supposition of his innocence. James was very properly unwilling to run the risk of protecting his Chancellor against the Parliament. But if the Chancellor had been able, by force of argument, to obtain an acquittal from the Parliament, we have no doubt that both the King and Villiers would have heartily rejoiced. They would have rejoiced, not merely on account of their friendship for Bacon, which seems, however, to have been as sincere as most friendships of that sort, but on selfish grounds. Nothing could have strengthened the government more than such a victory. The King and the favourite abandoned the Chancellor because they were unable to avert his disgrace, and unwilling to share it. Mr. Montagu mistakes effect for cause. He thinks that Bacon did not prove his innocence because he was not supported by the Court. The truth evidently is that the Court did not venture to support Bacon because he could not prove his innocence.

Again it seems strange that Mr. Montagu should not perceive that, while attempting to vindicate Bacon's reputation, he is really casting on it the foulest of all aspersions. He imputes to his idol a degree of meanness and depravity more loathsome than judicial corruption itself. A corrupt judge may have many good qualities. But a man who, to please a powerful patron, solemnly declares himself guilty of corruption when he knows himself to be innocent, must be a monster of servility and impudence. Bacon was, to say nothing of his highest claims to respect, a gentleman, a nobleman, a scholar, a statesman, a man of the first consideration in society, a man far advanced in years. Is it possible to believe that such a man would, to gratify any human being, irreparably ruin his own character by his own act? Imagine a grey-headed judge, full of years and honours, owning with tears, with pathetic assurances of his penitence and of his sincerity, that he has been guilty of shameful malpractices, repeatedly asseverating the truth of his confession, subscribing it with his own hand, submitting to conviction, receiving a humiliating sentence and acknowledging its justice, and all this when he has it in his power to show that his conduct has been irreproachable! The thing is incredible. But if we admit it to be true, what must we think of such a man, if indeed he deserves the name of man, who thinks anything that kings and minions can bestow more precious than honour, or anything that they can inflict more terrible than infamy.

Of this most disgraceful imputation we fully acquit Bacon. He had no defence; and Mr. Montagu's affectionate attempt to make a defence for him has altogether failed.

The grounds on which Mr. Montagu rests the case are two: the first, that the taking of presents was usual, and, what he seems to consider as the same thing, not discreditable; the second, that these presents were not taken as bribes.

Mr. Montagu brings forward many facts in support of his first proposition. He is not content with showing that many English judges formerly received gifts from suitors, but collects similar instances from foreign nations and ancient times. He goes back to the commonwealths of Greece, and attempts to press into his service a line of Homer and a sentence of Plutarch, which, we fear, will hardly serve his turn. The gold of which Homer speaks was not intended to fee the judges, but was paid into court for the benefit of the successful litigant; and the gratuities which Pericles, as Plutarch states, distributed among the members of the Athenian tribunals, were legal wages paid out of the public revenue. We can supply Mr. Montagu with passages much more in point. Hesiod, who, like poor Aubrey, had a "killing decree" made against him in the Chancery of Ascra, forgot decorum so far that he ventured to designate the learned persons who presided in that court as βασιλῆας δωροφάγους. Plutarch and Diodorus have handed down to the latest ages the respectable name of Anytus, the son of Anthemion, the first defendant who, eluding all the safeguards which the ingenuity of Solon could devise, succeeded in corrupting a bench of Athenian judges. We are indeed so far from grudging Mr. Montagu the aid of Greece, that we will give him Rome into the bargain. We acknowledge that the honourable senators who tried Verres received presents which were worth more than the fee-simple of York House and Gorhambury together, and that the no less honourable senators and knights who professed to believe in the *alibi* of Clodius obtained marks still more extraordinary of the esteem and gratitude of the defendant. In short, we are ready to admit that, before Bacon's time, and in Bacon's time, judges were in the habit of receiving gifts from suitors.

But is this a defence? We think not. The robberies of Cacus and Barabbas are no apology for those of Turpin. The conduct of the two men of Belial who swore away the life of Naboth has never been cited as an excuse for the perjuries of Oates and Dangerfield. Mr. Montagu has confounded two things which it is necessary carefully to distinguish from each other, if we wish to form a correct judgment of the characters of men of other countries and other times. That an immoral action is, in a particular society, generally considered as innocent, is a good plea for an individual who, being one of that society, and having adopted the notions which prevail among his neighbours, commits that action. But the circumstance that a great many people are in the habit of committing immoral actions is no plea at all. We should think it unjust to call St. Louis a wicked man, because, in an age in which toleration was generally regarded as a sin, he persecuted heretics. We should think it unjust to call Cowper's friend, John Newton, a hypocrite and a monster, because, at a time when the slave-trade was commonly considered by the most respectable people as an innocent and beneficial traffic, he went, largely provided with hymn-books and handcuffs, on a Guinea voyage. But the circumstance that there are twenty thousand thieves in London is no excuse for a fellow who is caught breaking into a shop. No man is to be blamed for not making discoveries in morality, for not finding out that something which everybody else thinks to be good is really bad. But, if a man does that which he and all around him know to be bad, it is no excuse for him that many others have done the same. We should be ashamed of spending so much time in pointing out so clear a distinction, but that Mr. Montagu seems altogether to overlook it.

Now, to apply these principles to the case before us; let Mr. Montagu prove that, in Bacon's age, the practices for which Bacon was punished were generally considered as innocent; and we admit that he has made out his point. But this we defy him to do. That these practices were common we admit. But they were common just as all wickedness to which there is strong temptation always was and always will be common. They were common just as theft, cheating, perjury, adultery have always been common. They were common, not because people did not know what was right, but because people liked to do what was wrong. They were common though prohibited by law. They were common, though condemned by public opinion. They were common, because in that age law and public opinion united had not sufficient force to restrain the greediness of powerful and unprincipled magistrates. They were common, as every crime will be common when the gain to which it leads is great, and the chance of punishment small. But, though common, they were universally allowed to be altogether unjustifiable; they were in the highest degree odious; and, though many were guilty of them, none had the audacity publicly to avow and defend them.

We could give a thousand proofs that the opinion then entertained concerning these practices was such as we have described. But we will content ourselves with calling a single witness, honest Hugh Latimer. His sermons, preached more than seventy years before the inquiry into Bacon's conduct, abound with the sharpest invectives against those very practices of which Bacon was guilty, and which, as Mr. Montagu seems to think, nobody ever considered as blamable till Bacon was punished for them. We could easily fill twenty pages with the homely, but just and forcible, rhetoric of the brave old bishop. We shall select a few passages as fair specimens, and no more than fair specimens, of the rest. "*Omnes diligunt munera.* They all love bribes. Bribery is a princely kind of thieving. They will be waged by the rich, either to give sentence against the poor, or to put off the poor man's cause. This is the noble theft of princes and magistrates. They are bribe-takers. Nowadays they call them gentle rewards. Let them leave their colouring, and call them by their Christian name—bribes." And again: "Cambyses was a great emperor, such another as our master is. He had many lord deputies, lord presidents, and lieutenants under him. It is a great while ago since I read the history. It chanced he had under him in one of his dominions a briber, a gift-taker, a gratifier of rich men; he followed gifts as fast as he that followed the pudding, a handmaker in his office to make his son a great man, as the old saying is: Happy is the child whose father goeth to the devil. The cry of the poor widow came to the emperor's ear, and caused him to flay the judge quick, and laid his skin in the chair of judgment, that all judges that should give judgment afterward should sit in the same skin. Surely it was a goodly sign, a goodly monument, the sign of the judge's skin. I pray God we may once see the skin in England." "I am sure," says he in another sermon, "this is *scala inferni*, the right way to hell, to be covetous, to take bribes, and pervert justice. If a

judge should ask me the way to hell, I would show him
this way. First, let him be a covetous man; let his
heart be poisoned with covetousness. Then let him go
a little further and take bribes; and, lastly, pervert
judgment. Lo, here is the mother, and the daughter,
and the daughter's daughter. Avarice is the mother:
she brings forth bribe-taking, and bribe-taking perverting of judgment. There lacks a fourth thing to make
up the mess, which, so help me God, if I were a judge,
should be *hangum tuum*, a Tyburn tippet to take with
him; an it were the judge of the King's bench, my
Lord Chief Judge of England, yea, an it were my Lord
Chancellor himself, to Tyburn with him." We will
quote but one more passage. "He that took the silver
basin and ewer for a bribe, thinketh that it will never
come out. But he may now know that I know it, and I
know it not alone; there be more beside me that know
it. Oh, briber and bribery! He was never a good
man that will so take bribes. Nor can I believe that he
that is a briber will be a good justice. It will never be
merry in England till we have the skins of such. For
what needeth bribing where men do their things up-
rightly?"

This was not the language of a great philosopher
who had made new discoveries in moral and political
science. It was the plain talk of a plain man, who
sprang from the body of the people, who sympathised
strongly with their wants and their feelings, and who

boldly uttered their opinions. It was on account of the fearless way in which stout-hearted old Hugh exposed the misdeeds of men in ermine tippets and gold collars, that the Londoners cheered him, as he walked down the Strand to preach at Whitehall, struggled for a touch of his gown, and bawled "Have at them, Father Latimer." It is plain, from the passages which we have quoted, and from fifty others which we might quote, that, long before Bacon was born, the accepting of presents by a judge was known to be a wicked and shameful act, that the fine words under which it was the fashion to veil such corrupt practices were even then seen through by the common people, that the distinction in which Mr. Montagu insists between compliments and bribes was even then laughed at as a mere colouring. There may be some oratorical exaggeration in what Latimer says about the Tyburn tippet and the sign of the judge's skin; but the fact that he ventured to use such expressions is amply sufficient to prove that the gift-taking judges, the receivers of silver basins and ewers, were regarded as such pests of the commonwealth that a venerable divine might, without any breach of Christian charity, publicly pray to God for their detection and their condign punishment.

Mr. Montagu tells us, most justly, that we ought not to transfer the opinions of our age to a former age. But he has himself committed a greater error than that against which he has cautioned his readers. Without any evidence, nay, in the face of the strongest evidence, he ascribes to the people of a former age a set of opinions which no people ever held. But any hypothesis is in his view more probable than that Bacon should have been a dishonest man. We firmly believe that, if papers were to be discovered which should irresistibly prove that Bacon was concerned in the poisoning of Sir Thomas Overbury, Mr. Montagu would tell us that, at the beginning of the seventeenth century, it was not thought improper in a man to put arsenic into the broth of his friends, and that we ought to blame, not Bacon, but the age in which he lived.

But why should we have recourse to any other evidence, when the proceeding against Lord Bacon is itself the best evidence on the subject? When Mr. Montagu tells us that we ought not to transfer the opinions of our age to Bacon's age, he appears altogether to forget that it was by men of Bacon's own age that Bacon was prosecuted, tried, convicted, and sentenced. Did not they know what their own opinions were? Did not they know whether they thought the taking of gifts by a judge a crime or not? Mr. Montagu complains bitterly that Bacon was induced to abstain from making a defence. But, if Bacon's defence resembled that which is made for him in the volume before us, it would have been unnecessary to trouble the Houses with it. The Lords and Commons did not want Bacon to tell them the thoughts of their own hearts, to inform them that they did not consider such practices as those in which they had detected him as at all culpable. Mr. Montagu's proposition may, indeed, be fairly stated thus:—It was very hard that Bacon's contemporaries should think it wrong in him to do what they did not think it wrong in him to do. Hard indeed, and withal somewhat improbable. Will any person say that the Commons who impeached Bacon for taking presents, and the Lords who sentenced him to fine, imprisonment, and degradation for taking presents, did not know that the taking of presents was a crime? Or, will any person say that Bacon did not know what the whole House of Commons and the whole House of Lords knew? Nobody who is not prepared to maintain one of these absurd propositions can deny that Bacon committed what he knew to be a crime.

It cannot be pretended that the Houses were seeking occasion to ruin Bacon, and that they therefore brought him to punishment on charges which they themselves knew to be frivolous. In no quarter was there the faintest indication of a disposition to treat him harshly. Through the whole proceeding there was no symptom of personal animosity or of factious violence in either House. Indeed, we will venture to say that no State trial in our history is more creditable to all who took part in it, either as prosecutors or judges. The decency, the gravity, the public spirit, the justice moderated but not unnerved by compassion, which appeared in every part of the transaction, would do honour to the most respectable public men of our own times. The accusers, while they discharged their duty to their constituents by bringing the misdeeds of the Chancellor to light, spoke with admiration of his many eminent qualities. The Lords, while condemning him, complimented him on the ingenuousness of his confession, and spared him the humiliation of a public appearance at their bar. So strong was the contagion of good feeling, that even Sir Edward Coke, for the first time in his life, behaved like a gentleman. No criminal ever had more temperate prosecutors than Bacon. No criminal ever had more favourable judges. If he was convicted, it was because it was impossible to acquit him without offering the grossest outrage to justice and common sense.

Mr. Montagu's other argument, namely, that Bacon, though he took gifts, did not take bribes, seems to us as futile as that which we have considered. Indeed, we might be content to leave it to be answered by the plainest man among our readers. Demosthenes noticed it with contempt more than two thousand years ago. Latimer, we have seen, treated this sophistry with similar disdain. "Leave colouring," said he, "and call these things by their Christian name, bribes." Mr. Montagu attempts, somewhat unfairly, we must say, to represent the presents which Bacon received as similar to the perquisites which suitors paid to the members of the Parliaments of France. The French magistrate had a legal right to his fee; and the amount of the fee was regulated by law. Whether this be a good mode of remunerating judges is not the question. But what analogy is there between payments of this sort and the presents which Bacon received, presents which were not sanctioned by the law, which were not made under the public eye, and of which the amount was regulated only by private bargain between the magistrate and the suitor?

Again, it is mere trifling to say that Bacon could not have meant to act corruptly, because he employed the agency of men of rank, of bishops, privy councillors, and members of parliament; as if the whole history of that generation was not full of the low actions of high people; as if it was not notorious that men, as exalted in rank as any of the decoys that Bacon employed, had pimped for Somerset, and poisoned Overbury.

But, says Mr. Montagu, these presents "were made openly, and with the greatest publicity." This would indeed be a strong argument in favour of Bacon. But we deny the fact. In one, and one only, of the cases in which Bacon was accused of corruptly receiving gifts does he appear to have received a gift publicly. This was in a matter depending between the Company of Apothecaries and the Company of Grocers. Bacon, in his Confession, insisted strongly on the circumstance that he had on this occasion taken a present publicly, as a proof that he had not taken it corruptly. Is it not clear that, if he had taken the presents mentioned in the other charges in the same public manner, he would have dwelt on this point in his answer to those charges? The fact that he insists so strongly on the publicity of one particular present is of itself sufficient to prove that the other presents were not publicly taken. Why he took this present publicly and the rest secretly is evident. He on that occasion acted openly, because he was acting honestly. He was not on that occasion sitting judicially. He was called in to effect an amicable arrangement between two parties. Both were satisfied with his decision. Both joined in making him a present in return for his trouble. Whether it was quite delicate in a man of his rank to accept a present under such circumstances may be questioned. But there is no ground in this case for accusing him of corruption.

Unhappily, the very circumstances which prove him to have been innocent in this case prove him to have been guilty on the other charges. Once, and once only, he alleges that he received a present publicly. The natural inference is that in all the other cases mentioned in the articles against him he received presents secretly. When we examine the single case in which he alleges that he received a present publicly, we find that it is also the single case in which there was no gross impropriety in his receiving a present. Is it then possible to doubt that his reason for not receiving other presents in as public a manner was that he knew that it was wrong to receive them?

One argument still remains, plausible in appearance, but admitting of easy and complete refutation. The two chief complainants, Aubrey and Egerton, had both made presents to the Chancellor. But he had decided against them both. Therefore, he had not received those presents as bribes. "The complaints of his accusers were," says Mr. Montagu, "not that the gratuities had, but that they had not influenced Bacon's judgment, as he had decided against them."

The truth is, that it is precisely in this way that an extensive system of corruption is generally detected. A person who, by a bribe, has procured a decree in his favour is by no means likely to come forward of his own accord as an accuser. He is content. He has his *quid pro quo*. He is not impelled either by interested or by vindictive motives to bring the transaction before the public. On the contrary, he has almost as strong motives for holding his tongue as the judge himself can have. But when a judge practises corruption, as we fear that Bacon practised it, on a large scale, and has many agents looking out in different quarters for prey, it will sometimes happen that he will be bribed on both sides. It will sometimes happen that he will receive money from suitors who are so obviously in the wrong that he cannot with decency do anything to serve them. Thus he will now and then be forced to pronounce against a person from whom he has received a present; and he makes that person a deadly enemy. The hundreds who have got what they paid for remain quiet. It is the two or three who have paid, and have nothing to show for their money, who are noisy.

The memorable example of the Goëzmans is an example of this. Beaumarchais had an important suit depending before the Parliament of Paris. M. Goëzman was the judge on whom chiefly the decision depended. It was hinted to Beaumarchais that Madame Goëzman might be propitiated by a present. He accordingly offered a purse of gold to the lady, who received it graciously. There can be no doubt that, if the decision of the court had been favourable to him, these things would never have been known to the world. But he lost his cause. Almost the whole sum which he had expended in bribery was immediately refunded; and those who had disappointed him probably thought that he would not, for the mere gratification of his malevolence, make public a transaction which was discreditable to himself as well as to them. They knew little of him. He soon taught them to curse the day in which they had dared to trifle with a man of so revengeful and turbulent a spirit, of such dauntless effrontery, and of such eminent talents for controversy and satire. He compelled the Parliament to put a degrading stigma on M. Goëzman. He drove Madame Goëzman to a convent. Till it was too late to pause, his excited passions did not suffer him to remember that he could effect their ruin only by disclosures ruinous to himself. We could give other instances. But it is needless. No person well acquainted with human nature can fail to perceive that, if the doctrine for which Mr. Montagu contends were admitted, society would be deprived of almost the only chance which it has of detecting the corrupt practices of judges.

We return to our narrative. The sentence of Bacon had scarcely been pronounced when it was mitigated. He was indeed sent to the Tower. But this was merely a form. In two days he was set at liberty, and soon after he retired to Gorhambury. His fine was speedily released by the Crown. He was next suffered to present himself at Court; and at length, in 1624, the rest of his punishment was remitted. He was now at liberty to resume his seat in the House of Lords, and he was actually summoned to the next Parliament. But age, infirmity, and perhaps shame, prevented him from attending. The Government allowed him a pension of twelve hundred pounds a year; and his whole annual income is estimated by Mr. Montagu at two thousand five hundred pounds, a sum which was probably above the average income of a nobleman of that generation, and which was certainly sufficient for comfort and even for splendour. Unhappily, Bacon was fond of display, and unused to pay minute attention to domestic affairs. He was not easily persuaded to give up any part of the magnificence to which he had been accustomed in the time of his power and prosperity. No pressure of distress could induce him to part with the woods of Gorhambury. "I will not," he said, "be stripped of my feathers." He travelled with so splendid an equipage and so large a retinue that Prince Charles, who once fell in with him on the road, exclaimed with surprise, "Well; do what we can, this man scorns to go out in snuff." This carelessness and ostentation reduced Bacon to frequent distress. He was under the necessity of parting with York House, and of taking up his residence, during his visits to London, at his old chambers in Gray's Inn. He had other vexations, the exact nature of which is unknown. It is evident from his will that some part of his wife's conduct had greatly disturbed and irritated him.

But, whatever might be his pecuniary difficulties or his conjugal discomforts, the powers of his intellect still remained undiminished. Those noble studies for which he had found leisure in the midst of professional drudgery and of courtly intrigues gave to this last sad stage of his life a dignity beyond what power or titles could bestow. Impeached, convicted, sentenced, driven with ignominy from the presence of his Sovereign, shut out from the deliberations of his fellow nobles, loaded with debt, branded with dishonour, sinking under the weight of years, sorrows, and diseases, Bacon was Bacon still. "My conceit of his person," says Ben Jonson very finely, "was never increased towards him by his place or honours; but I have and do reverence him for the greatness that was only proper to himself; in that he seemed to me ever, by his work, one of the greatest men and most worthy of admiration that had been in many ages. In his adversity I ever prayed that God would give him strength; for greatness he could not want."

The services which Bacon rendered to letters during the last five years of his life, amidst ten thousand distractions and vexations, increase the regret with which we think on the many years which he had wasted, to use the words of Sir Thomas Bodley, "on such study as was not worthy of such a student." He commenced a Digest of the Laws of England, a History of England under the Princes of the House of Tudor, a body of Natural History, a Philosophical Romance. He made extensive and valuable additions to his Essays. He published the inestimable Treatise *De Augmentis Scientiarum*. The very trifles with which he amused himself in hours of pain and languor bore the mark of his mind. The best collection of jests in the world is that which he dictated from memory.

without referring to any book, on a day on which illness had rendered him incapable of serious study.

The great apostle of experimental philosophy was destined to be its martyr. It had occurred to him that snow might be used with advantage for the purpose of preventing animal substances from putrefying. On a very cold day, early in the spring of the year 1626, he alighted from his coach near Highgate, in order to try the experiment. He went into a cottage, bought a fowl, and with his own hands stuffed it with snow. While thus engaged he felt a sudden chill, and was soon so much indisposed that it was impossible for him to return to Gray's Inn. The Earl of Arundel, with whom he was well acquainted, had a house at Highgate. To that house Bacon was carried. The Earl was absent; but the servants who were in charge of the place showed great respect and attention to the illustrious guest. Here, after an illness of about a week, he expired early on the morning of Easter Day, 1626. His mind appears to have retained its strength and liveliness to the end. He did not forget the fowl which had caused his death. In the last letter that he ever wrote, with fingers which, as he said, could not steadily hold a pen, he did not omit to mention that the experiment of the snow had succeeded "excellently well."

Our opinion of the moral character of this great man has already been sufficiently explained. Had his life been passed in literary retirement, he would, in all probability, have deserved to be considered, not only as a great philosopher, but as a worthy and good-natured member of society. But neither his principles nor his spirit were such as could be trusted, when strong temptations were to be resisted, and serious dangers to be braved.

In his will he expressed with singular brevity, energy, dignity, and pathos, a mournful consciousness that his actions had not been such as to entitle him to the esteem of those under whose observation his life had been passed, and, at the same time, a proud confidence that his writings had secured for him a high and permanent place among the benefactors of mankind. So at least we understand those striking words which have been often quoted, but which we must quote once more: "For my name and memory, I leave it to men's charitable speeches, and to foreign nations, and to the next age."

His confidence was just. From the day of his death his fame has been constantly and steadily progressive; and we have no doubt that his name will be named with reverence to the latest ages, and to the remotest ends of the civilised world.

The chief peculiarity of Bacon's philosophy seems to us to have been this, that it aimed at things altogether different from those which his predecessors had proposed to themselves. This was his own opinion.

"*Finis scientiarum*," says he, "*a nemine adhuc bene positus est.*" And again, "*Omnium gravissimus error in deviatione ab ultimo doctrinarum fine consistit.*" "*Nec ipsa meta*," says he elsewhere, "*adhuc ulli, quod sciam, mortalium posita est et defixa.*" The more carefully his works are examined, the more clearly, we think, it will appear that this is the real clue to his whole system, and that he used means different from those used by other philosophers, because he wished to arrive at an end altogether different from theirs.

What, then, was the end which Bacon proposed to himself? It was, to use his own emphatic expression, "fruit." It was the multiplying of human enjoyments and the mitigating of human sufferings. It was "the relief of man's estate." It was "*commodis humanis inservire.*" It was "*efficaciter operari ad sublevanda vitæ humanæ incommoda.*" It was "*dotare vitam humanam novis inventis et copiis.*" It was "*genus humanum novis operibus et potestatibus continuo dotare.*" This was the object of all his speculations in every department of science, in natural philosophy, in legislation, in politics, in morals.

Two words form the key of the Baconian doctrine, Utility and Progress. The ancient philosophy disdained to be useful, and was content to be stationary. It dealt largely in theories of moral perfection, which were so sublime that they never could be more than theories; in attempts to solve insoluble enigmas; in exhortations to the attainment of unattainable frames of mind. It could not condescend to the humble office of ministering to the comfort of human beings. All the schools contemned that office as degrading; some censured it as immoral. Once indeed Posidonius, a distinguished writer of the age of Cicero and Cæsar, so far forgot himself as to enumerate, among the humbler blessings which mankind owed to philosophy, the discovery of the principle of the arch, and the introduction of the use of metals. This eulogy was considered as an affront, and was taken up with proper spirit. Seneca vehemently disclaims these insulting compliments. Philosophy, according to him, has nothing to do with teaching men to rear arched roofs over their heads. The true philosopher does not care whether he has an arched roof or any roof. Philosophy has nothing to do with teaching men the uses of metals. She teaches us to be independent of all material substances, of all mechanical contrivances. The wise man lives according to nature. Instead of attempting to add to the physical comforts of his species, he regrets that his lot was not cast in that golden age when the human race had no protection against the cold but the skins of wild beasts, no screen from the sun but a cavern. To impute to such a man any share in the invention or improvement of a plough, a ship, or a mill, is an insult. "In my own time," says Seneca, "there have been inventions of this sort—transparent windows, tubes for diffusing warmth equally through all parts of a building, short-hand, which has been carried to such a perfection that a writer can keep pace with the most rapid speaker. But the inventing of such things is drudgery for the lowest slaves; philosophy lies deeper. It is not her office to teach men how to use their hands. The object of her lessons is to form the soul. *Non est, inquam, instrumentorum ad usus necessarios opifex.*" If the *non* were left out, this last sentence would be no bad description of the Baconian philosophy, and would, indeed, very much resemble several expressions in the *Novum Organum.* "We shall next be told," exclaims Seneca, "that the first shoemaker was a philosopher." For our own part, if we are forced to make our choice between the first shoemaker and the author of the three books On Anger, we pronounce for the shoemaker. It may be worse to be angry than to be wet. But shoes have kept millions from being wet; and we doubt whether Seneca ever kept anybody from being angry.

It is very reluctantly that Seneca can be brought to confess that any philosopher had ever paid the smallest attention to anything that could possibly promote what vulgar people would consider as the well-being of mankind. He labours to clear Democritus from the disgraceful imputation of having made the first arch, and Anacharsis from the charge of having contrived the potter's wheel. He is forced to own that such a thing might happen; and it may also happen, he tells us, that a philosopher may be swift of foot. But it is not in his character of philosopher that he either wins a race or invents a machine. No, to be sure. The business of a philosopher was to declaim in praise of poverty with two millions sterling out at usury, to meditate epigrammatic conceits about the evils of luxury, in gardens which moved the envy of sovereigns, to rant about liberty, while fawning on the insolent and pampered freedmen of a tyrant, to celebrate the divine beauty of virtue with the same pen which had just before written a defence of the murder of a mother by a son.

From the cant of this philosophy, a philosophy meanly proud of its own unprofitableness, it is delightful to turn to the lessons of the great English teacher. We can almost forgive all the faults of Bacon's life when we read that singularly graceful and dignified passage: "*Ego certe, ut de me ipso, quod res est, loquar, et in iis quæ nunc edo, et in iis quæ in posterum meditor, dignitatem ingenii et nominis mei, si qua sit, sæpius sciens et volens projicio, dum commodis humanis inserviam; quique architectus fortasse in philosophia et scientiis esse debeam, etiam operarius, et bajulus, et quidvis demum fio, cum haud pauca quæ omnino fieri necesse sit, alii autem ob innatam superbiam subterfugiant, ipse sustineam et exsequar.*" This *philanthropia*, which, as he said in one of the most remarkable of his early letters, "was so fixed in his mind as it could not be removed," this majestic humility, this persuasion that nothing can be too insignificant for the attention of the wisest, which is not too insignificant to give pleasure or pain to the meanest, is the great characteristic distinction, the essential spirit of the Baconian philosophy. We trace it in all that Bacon has written on Physics, on Laws, on Morals. And we conceive that from this peculiarity all the other peculiarities of his system directly and almost necessarily sprang.

The spirit which appears in the passage of Seneca to which we have referred tainted the whole body of the ancient philosophy from the time of Socrates downwards, and took possession of intellects with which that of Seneca cannot for a moment be compared. It pervades the dialogues of Plato. It may be distinctly traced in many parts of the works of Aristotle. Bacon has dropped hints from which it may be inferred that, in his opinion, the prevalence of this feeling was in a great measure to be attributed to the influence of Socrates. Our great countryman evidently did not consider the revolution which Socrates effected in philosophy as a happy event, and constantly maintained that the earlier Greek speculators, Democritus in particular, were, on the whole, superior to their more celebrated successors.

Assuredly, if the tree which Socrates planted and

Plato watered is to be judged of by its flowers and leaves, it is the noblest of trees. But if we take the homely test of Bacon, if we judge of the tree by its fruits, our opinion of it may perhaps be less favourable. When we sum up all the useful truths which we owe to that philosophy, to what do they amount? We find, indeed, abundant proofs that some of those who cultivated it were men of the first order of intellect. We find among their writings incomparable specimens both of dialectical and rhetorical art. We have no doubt that the ancient controversies were of use, in so far as they served to exercise the faculties of the disputants; for there is no controversy so idle that it may not be of use in this way. But, when we look for something more, for something which adds to the comforts or alleviates the calamities of the human race, we are forced to own ourselves disappointed. We are forced to say with Bacon that this celebrated philosophy ended in nothing but disputation, that it was neither a vineyard nor an olive-ground, but an intricate wood of briers and thistles, from which those who lost themselves in it brought back many scratches and no food.

We readily acknowledge that some of the teachers of this unfruitful wisdom were among the greatest men that the world has ever seen. If we admit the justice of Bacon's censure, we admit it with regret, similar to that which Dante felt when he learned the

fate of those illustrious heathens who were doomed to
the first circle of Hell.

> "Gran duol mi prese al cuor quando lo 'ntesi,
> Perocché gente di molto valore
> Conobbi che 'n quel limbo eran sospesi."

But, in truth, the very admiration which we feel for
the eminent philosophers of antiquity forces us to
adopt the opinion that their powers were systematically
misdirected. For how else could it be that such
powers should effect so little for mankind? A pedes-
trian may show as much muscular vigour on a treadmill as on the highway road. But on the road his
vigour will assuredly carry him forward; and on the
treadmill he will not advance an inch. The ancient
philosophy was a treadmill, not a path. It was made
up of revolving questions, of controversies which
were always beginning again. It was a contrivance
for having much exertion and no progress. We must
acknowledge that more than once, while contemplating
the doctrines of the Academy and the Portico, even as
they appear in the transparent splendour of Cicero's
incomparable diction, we have been tempted to mutter
with the surly centurion in Persius, "*Cur quis non
prandeat, hoc est?*" What is the highest good,
whether pain be an evil, whether all things be fated,
whether we can be certain of anything, whether we

can be certain that we are certain of nothing, whether a wise man can be unhappy, whether all departures from right be equally reprehensible—these, and other questions of the same sort, occupied the brains, the tongues, and the pens of the ablest men in the civilised world during several centuries. This sort of philosophy, it is evident, could not be progressive. It might indeed sharpen and invigorate the minds of those who devoted themselves to it; and so might the disputes of the orthodox Lilliputians and the heretical Blefuscudians about the big ends and the little ends of eggs. But such disputes could add nothing to the stock of knowledge. The human mind, accordingly, instead of marching, merely marked time. It took as much trouble as would have sufficed to carry it forward; and yet remained on the same spot. There was no accumulation of truth, no heritage of truth acquired by the labour of one generation and bequeathed to another, to be again transmitted with large additions to a third. Where this philosophy was in the time of Cicero, there it continued to be in the time of Seneca, and there it continued to be in the time of Favorinus. The same sects were still battling, with the same unsatisfactory arguments, about the same interminable questions. There had been no want of ingenuity, of zeal, of industry. Every trace of intellectual cultivation was there, except a harvest. There had been plenty of ploughing, harrowing, reaping, threshing. But the garners contained only smut and stubble.

The ancient philosophers did not neglect natural science; but they did not cultivate it for the purpose of increasing the power and ameliorating the condition of man. The taint of barrenness had spread from ethical to physical speculations. Seneca wrote largely on natural philosophy, and magnified the importance of that study. But why? Not because it tended to assuage suffering, to multiply the conveniences of life, to extend the empire of man over the material world; but solely because it tended to raise the mind above low cares, to separate it from the body, to exercise its subtilty in the solution of very obscure questions. Thus natural philosophy was considered in the light merely of a mental exercise. It was made subsidiary to the art of disputation; and it consequently proved altogether barren of useful discoveries.

There was one sect which, however absurd and pernicious some of its doctrines may have been, ought, it should seem, to have merited an exception from the general censure which Bacon has pronounced on the ancient schools of wisdom. The Epicurean who referred all happiness to bodily pleasure, and all evil to bodily pain, might have been expected to exert himself for the purpose of bettering his own physical condition and that of his neighbours. But the thought seems never to have occurred to any member of that school. Indeed, their notion, as reported by their great poet, was, that no more improvements were to be expected in the arts which conduce to the comfort of life.

> "Ad victum quæ flagitat usus
> Omnia jam ferme mortalibus esse parata."

This contented despondency, this disposition to admire what has been done, and to expect that nothing more will be done, is strongly characteristic of all the schools which preceded the school of Fruit and Progress. Widely as the Epicurean and the Stoic differed on most points, they seem to have quite agreed in their contempt for pursuits so vulgar as to be useful. The philosophy of both was a garrulous, declaiming, canting, wrangling philosophy. Century after century they continued to repeat their hostile war-cries, Virtue and Pleasure; and in the end it appeared that the Epicurean had added as little to the quantity of pleasure as the Stoic to the quantity of virtue. It is on the pedestal of Bacon, not on that of Epicurus, that those noble lines ought to be inscribed:

> "O tenebris tantis tam clarum extollere lumen
> Qui primus potuisti, illustrans commoda vitæ."

In the fifth century Christianity had conquered Paganism, and Paganism had infected Christianity. The Church was now victorious and corrupt. The rites of the Pantheon had passed into her worship, the subtilties of the Academy into her creed. In an evil day, though with great pomp and solemnity—we quote the language of Bacon—was the ill-starred alliance stricken between the old philosophy and the new faith. Questions widely different from those which had employed the ingenuity of Pyrrho and Carneades, but just as subtle, just as interminable, and just as unprofitable, exercised the minds of the lively and voluble Greeks. When learning began to revive in the West, similar trifles occupied the sharp and vigorous intellects of the Schoolmen. There was another sowing of the wind, and another reaping of the whirlwind. The great work of improving the condition of the human race was still considered as unworthy of a man of learning. Those who undertook that task, if what they effected could be readily comprehended, were despised as mechanics; if not, they were in danger of being burned as conjurers.

There cannot be a stronger proof of the degree in which the human mind had been misdirected than the history of the two greatest events which took place during the middle ages. We speak of the invention of gunpowder and of the invention of printing. The dates of both are unknown. The authors of both are unknown. Nor was this because men were too rude and ignorant to value intellectual superiority. The inventor of gunpowder appears to have been contemporary with Petrarch and Boccaccio. The inventor of printing was certainly contemporary with Nicholas the Fifth, with Cosmo de' Medici, and with a crowd of distinguished scholars. But the human mind still retained that fatal bent which it had received two thousand years earlier. George of Trebisond and Marsilio Ficino would not easily have been brought to believe that the inventor of the printing-press had done more for mankind than themselves, or than those ancient writers of whom they were the enthusiastic votaries.

At length the time arrived when the barren philosophy which had, during so many ages, employed the faculties of the ablest of men, was destined to fall. It had worn many shapes. It had mingled itself with many creeds. It had survived revolutions in which empires, religions, languages, races, had perished. Driven from its ancient haunts, it had taken sanctuary in that Church which it had persecuted, and had, like the daring fiends of the poet, placed its seat

"Next the seat of God,
And with its darkness dared affront his light."

Words, and more words, and nothing but words, had been all the fruit of all the toil of all the most renowned sages of sixty generations. But the days of this sterile exuberance were numbered.

Many causes predisposed the public mind to a change. The study of a great variety of ancient writers, though it did not give a right direction to philosophical research, did much towards destroying that blind reverence for authority which had prevailed when Aristotle ruled alone. The rise of the Florentine sect of Platonists, a sect to which belonged some of the finest minds of the fifteenth century, was not an unimportant event. The mere substitution of the Academic for the Peripatetic philosophy would indeed have done little good. But anything was better than the old habit of unreasoning servility. It was something to have a choice of tyrants. "A spark of freedom," as Gibbon has justly remarked, "was produced by this collision of adverse servitude."

Other causes might be mentioned. But it is chiefly to the great reformation of religion that we owe the great reformation of philosophy. The alliance between the Schools and the Vatican had for ages been so close, that those who threw off the dominion of the Vatican could not continue to recognise the authority of the Schools. Most of the chiefs of the schism treated the Peripatetic philosophy with contempt, and spoke of Aristotle as if Aristotle had been answerable for all the dogmas of Thomas Aquinas. "*Nullo apud Lutheranos philosophiam esse in pretio,*" was a reproach which the defenders of the Church of Rome loudly repeated, and which many of the Protestant leaders considered as a compliment. Scarcely any text was more frequently cited by the reformers than that in which St. Paul cautions the Colossians not to let any man spoil them by philosophy. Luther, almost at the outset of his career, went so far as to declare that no man could be at once a proficient in the school of Aristotle and in that of Christ. Zwingle, Bucer, Peter Martyr, Calvin, held similar language. In some of the Scotch universities, the Aristotelian system was discarded for that of Ramus. Thus, before the birth of Bacon, the empire of the scholastic philosophy had been shaken to its foundations. There was in the intellectual world an anarchy resembling that which in the political world often follows the overthrow of an old and deeply rooted government. Antiquity, prescription, the sound of great names, had ceased to awe mankind. The dynasty which had reigned for ages was at an end; and the vacant throne was left to be struggled for by pretenders.

The first effect of this great revolution was, as Bacon most justly observed, to give for a time an undue importance to the mere graces of style. The new breed of scholars, the Aschams and Buchanans, nourished with the finest compositions of the Augustan age, regarded with loathing the dry, crabbed, and barbarous diction of respondents and opponents. They were far less studious about the matter of their writing than about the manner. They succeeded in reforming

Latinity; but they never even aspired to effect a reform in philosophy.

At this time Bacon appeared. It is altogether incorrect to say, as has often been said, that he was the first man who rose up against the Aristotelian philosophy when in the height of its power. The authority of that philosophy had, as we have shown, received a fatal blow long before he was born. Several speculators, among whom Ramus is the best known, had recently attempted to form new sects. Bacon's own expressions about the state of public opinion in the time of Luther are clear and strong: "*Accedebat,*" says he, "*odium et contemptus, illis ipsis temporibus ortus erga Scholasticos.*" And again, "*Scholasticorum doctrina despectui prorsus haberi cœpit tanquam aspera et barbara.*" The part which Bacon played in this great change was the part, not of Robespierre, but of Bonaparte. The ancient order of things had been subverted. Some bigots still cherished with devoted loyalty the remembrance of the fallen monarchy, and exerted themselves to effect a restoration. But the majority had no such feeling. Freed, yet not knowing how to use their freedom, they pursued no determinate course, and had found no leader capable of conducting them.

That leader at length arose. The philosophy which he taught was essentially new. It differed from that of the celebrated ancient teachers, not merely in method, but also in object. Its object was the good of mankind, in the sense in which the mass of mankind always have understood and always will understand the word good. "*Meditor,*" said Bacon, "*instaurationem philosophiæ ejusmodi quæ nihil inanis aut abstracti habeat, quæque vitæ humanæ conditiones in melius provehat.*"

The difference between the philosophy of Bacon and that of his predecessors cannot, we think, be better illustrated than by comparing his views on some important subjects with those of Plato. We select Plato, because we conceive that he did more than any other person towards giving to the minds of speculative men that bent which they retained till they received from Bacon a new impulse in a diametrically opposite direction.

It is curious to observe how differently these great men estimated the value of every kind of knowledge. Take arithmetic, for example. Plato, after speaking slightly of the convenience of being able to reckon and compute in the ordinary transactions of life, passes to what he considers as a far more important advantage. The study of the properties of numbers, he tells us, habituates the mind to the contemplation of pure truth, and raises us above the material universe. He would have his disciples apply themselves to this study, not that they may be able to buy or sell, not that they may qualify themselves to be shopkeepers or travelling merchants, but that they may learn to withdraw their minds from the ever-shifting spectacle of this visible and tangible world, and to fix them on the immutable essences of things.

Bacon, on the other hand, valued this branch of knowledge, only on account of its uses with reference to that visible and tangible world which Plato so much despised. He speaks with scorn of the mystical arithmetic of the later Platonists, and laments the propensity of mankind to employ, on mere matters of curiosity, powers the whole exertion of which is required for purposes of solid advantage. He advises arithmeticians to leave these trifles, and to employ themselves in framing convenient expressions, which may be of use in physical researches.

The same reasons which led Plato to recommend the study of arithmetic led him to recommend also the study of mathematics. The vulgar crowd of geometricians, he says, will not understand him. They have practice always in view. They do not know that the real use of the science is to lead men to the knowledge of abstract, essential, eternal truth. Indeed, if we are to believe Plutarch, Plato carried this feeling so far that he considered geometry as degraded by being applied to any purpose of vulgar utility. Archytas, it seems, had framed machines of extraordinary power on mathematical principles. Plato remonstrated with his friend, and declared that this was to degrade a noble intellectual exercise into a low craft, fit only for carpenters and wheelwrights. The office of geometry, he said, was to discipline the mind, not to minister to the base wants of the body. His interference was successful; and from that time, according to Plutarch, the science of mechanics was considered as unworthy of the attention of a philosopher.

Archimedes in a later age imitated and surpassed Archytas. But even Archimedes was not free from the prevailing notion that geometry was degraded by being employed to produce anything useful. It was with difficulty that he was induced to stoop from speculation to practice. He was half ashamed of those inventions which were the wonder of hostile nations, and always spoke of them slightingly as mere amusements, as trifles in which a mathematician might be suffered to relax his mind after intense application to the higher parts of his science.

The opinion of Bacon on this subject was diametrically opposed to that of the ancient philosophers. He valued geometry chiefly, if not solely, on account of those uses, which to Plato appeared so base. And it is remarkable that the longer Bacon lived the stronger this feeling became. When in 1605 he wrote the two books on the Advancement of Learning, he dwelt on the advantages which mankind derived from mixed mathematics; but he at the same time admitted that the beneficial effect produced by mathematical study on the intellect, though a collateral advantage, was "no less worthy than that which was principal and intended." But it is evident that his views underwent a change. When, near twenty years later, he published the *De Augmentis,* which is the Treatise on the Advancement of Learning, greatly expanded and carefully corrected, he made important alterations in the part which related to mathematics. He condemned with severity the high pretensions of the mathematicians, "*delicias et fastum mathematicorum.*" Assuming the well-being of the human race to be the end of knowledge, he pronounced that mathematical science could claim no higher rank than that of an appendage or an auxiliary to other sciences. Mathematical science, he says, is the handmaid of natural philosophy; she ought to demean herself as such; and he declares that he cannot conceive by what ill chance it has happened that she presumes to claim precedence over her mistress. He predicts—a prediction which would have made Plato shudder—that as more and more discoveries are made in physics, there will be more and more branches of mixed mathematics. Of that collateral advantage, the value of which, twenty years before, he rated so highly, he says not one word. This omission cannot have been the effect of mere inadvertence. His own treatise was before him. From that treatise he deliberately expunged whatever was favourable to the study of pure mathematics, and inserted several keen reflections on the ardent votaries of that study. This fact, in our opinion, admits of only one explanation. Bacon's love of those pursuits which directly tend to improve the condition of mankind, and his jealousy of all pursuits merely curious, had grown upon him, and had, it may be, become immoderate. He was afraid of using any expression which might have the effect of inducing any man of talents to employ in speculations, useful only to the mind of the speculator, a single hour which might be employed in extending the empire of man over matter. If Bacon erred here, we must acknowledge that we greatly prefer his error to the opposite error of Plato. We have no patience with a philosophy which, like those Roman matrons who swallowed abortives in order to preserve their shapes, takes pains to be barren for fear of being homely.

Let us pass to astronomy. This was one of the sciences which Plato exhorted his disciples to learn, but for reasons far removed from common habits of thinking. "Shall we set down astronomy," says Socrates, "among the subjects of study?" "I think so," answers his young friend Glaucon: "to know something about the seasons, the months, and the years is of use for military purposes, as well as for agriculture and navigation." "It amuses me," says Socrates, "to see how afraid you are, lest the common herd of people should accuse you of recommending useless studies." He then proceeds, in that pure and magnificent diction which, as Cicero said, Jupiter would use if Jupiter spoke Greek, to explain, that the use of astronomy is not to add to the vulgar comforts of life, but to assist in raising the mind to the contemplation of things which are to be perceived by the pure intellect alone. The knowledge of the actual motions of the heavenly bodies Socrates considers as of little value. The appearances which make the sky beautiful at night are, he tells us, like the figures which a geometrician draws on the sand, mere examples, mere helps to feeble minds. We must get beyond them; we must neglect them; we must attain to an astronomy which is as independent of the actual stars as geometrical truth is independent of the lines of an ill-drawn diagram. This is, we imagine, very nearly, if not exactly, the astronomy which Bacon compared to the ox of Prometheus, a sleek, well-shaped hide, stuffed with rubbish, goodly to look at, but containing nothing to eat. He complained that astronomy had, to its great injury, been separated from natural philosophy, of which it was one of the noblest provinces, and annexed to the domain of mathematics. The world stood in need, he said, of a very different astronomy, of a living astronomy, of an astronomy which should set forth the nature, the motion, and the influences of the heavenly bodies, as they really are.

On the greatest and most useful of all human

inventions, the invention of alphabetical writing, Plato did not look with much complacency. He seems to have thought that the use of letters had operated on the human mind as the use of the go-cart in learning to walk, or of corks in learning to swim, is said to operate on the human body. It was a support which, in his opinion, soon became indispensable to those who used it, which made vigorous exertion first unnecessary, and then impossible. The powers of the intellect would, he conceived, have been more fully developed without this delusive aid. Men would have been compelled to exercise the understanding and the memory, and, by deep and assiduous meditation, to make truth thoroughly their own. Now, on the contrary, much knowledge is traced on paper, but little is engraved in the soul. A man is certain that he can find information at a moment's notice when he wants it. He therefore suffers it to fade from his mind. Such a man cannot in strictness be said to know anything. He has the show without the reality of wisdom. These opinions Plato has put into the mouth of an ancient king of Egypt. But it is evident from the context that they were his own; and so they were understood to be by Quinctilian. Indeed, they are in perfect accordance with the whole Platonic system.

Bacon's views, as may easily be supposed, were widely different. The powers of the memory, he observes, without the help of writing, can do little towards the advancement of any useful science. He acknowledges that the memory may be disciplined to such a point as to be able to perform very extraordinary feats. But on such feats he sets little value. The habits of his mind, he tells us, are such that he is not disposed to rate highly any accomplishment, however rare, which is of no practical use to mankind. As to these prodigious achievements of the memory, he ranks them with the exhibitions of rope-dancers and tumblers. "The two performances," he says, "are of much the same sort. The one is an abuse of the powers of the body; the other is an abuse of the powers of the mind. Both may perhaps excite our wonder; but neither is entitled to our respect."

To Plato, the science of medicine appeared to be of very disputable advantage. He did not, indeed, object to quick cures for acute disorders, or for injuries produced by accidents. But the art which resists the slow sap of a chronic disease, which repairs frames enervated by lust, swollen by gluttony, or inflamed by wine, which encourages sensuality by mitigating the natural punishment of the sensualist, and prolongs existence when the intellect has ceased to retain its entire energy, had no share of his esteem. A life protracted by medical skill he pronounced to be a long death. The exercise of the art of medicine ought, he said, to be tolerated, so far as that art may serve to cure the occasional distempers of men whose constitutions are good. As to those who have bad constitutions, let them die; and the sooner the better. Such men are unfit for war, for magistracy, for the management of their domestic affairs, for severe study and speculation. If they engage in any vigorous mental exercise, they are troubled with giddiness and fulness of the head, all which they lay to the account of philosophy. The best thing that can happen to such wretches is to have done with life at once. He quotes mythical authority in support of this doctrine: and reminds his disciples that the practice of the sons of Æsculapius, as described by Homer, extended only to the cure of external injuries.

Far different was the philosophy of Bacon. Of all the sciences, that which he seems to have regarded with the greatest interest was the science which, in Plato's opinion, would not be tolerated in a well-regulated community. To make men perfect was no part of Bacon's plan. His humble aim was to make imperfect men comfortable. The beneficence of his philosophy resembled the beneficence of the common Father, whose sun rises on the evil and the good, whose rain descends for the just and the unjust. In Plato's opinion man was made for philosophy: in Bacon's opinion philosophy was made for man; it was a means to an end; and that end was to increase the pleasures and to mitigate the pains of millions who are not and cannot be philosophers. That a valetudinarian

who took great pleasure in being wheeled along his
terrace, who relished his boiled chicken and his weak
wine and water, and who enjoyed a hearty laugh over
the Queen of Navarre's tales, should be treated as a
caput lupinum because he could not read the Timæus
without a headache, was a notion which the humane
spirit of the English school of wisdom altogether rejected. Bacon would not have thought it beneath the
dignity of a philosopher to contrive an improved
garden chair for such a valetudinarian, to devise some
way of rendering his medicines more palatable, to
invent repasts which he might enjoy, and pillows on
which he might sleep soundly; and this, though there
might not be the smallest hope that the mind of the
poor invalid would ever rise to the contemplation of
the ideal beautiful and the ideal good. As Plato had
cited the religious legends of Greece to justify his
contempt for the more recondite parts of the art of
healing, Bacon vindicated the dignity of that art by
appealing to the example of Christ, and reminded men
that the great Physician of the soul did not disdain to
be also the physician of the body.

When we pass from the science of medicine to that
of legislation, we find the same difference between the
systems of these two great men. Plato, at the com-
mencement of the Dialogue on Laws, lays it down as a
fundamental principle that the end of legislation is to
make men virtuous. It is unnecessary to point out the

extravagant conclusions to which such a proposition leads. Bacon well knew to how great an extent the happiness of every society must depend on the virtue of its members; and he also knew what legislators can and what they cannot do for the purpose of promoting virtue. The view which he has given of the end of legislation, and of the principal means for the attainment of that end, has always seemed to us eminently happy, even among the many happy passages of the same kind with which his works abound. "*Finis et scopus quem leges intueri atque ad quem jussiones et sanctiones suas dirigere debent, non alius est quam ut cives feliciter degant. Id fiet si pietate et religione recte instituti, moribus honesti, armis adversus hostes externos tuti, legum auxilio adversus seditiones et privatas injurias muniti, imperio et magistratibus obsequentes, copiis et opibus locupletes et florentes fuerint.*" The end is the well-being of the people. The means are the imparting of moral and religious education; the providing of everything necessary for defence against foreign enemies; the maintaining of internal order; the establishing of a judicial, financial, and commercial system, under which wealth may be rapidly accumulated and securely enjoyed.

Even with respect to the form in which laws ought to be drawn, there is a remarkable difference of opinion between the Greek and the Englishman.

Plato thought a preamble essential; Bacon thought it mischievous. Each was consistent with himself. Plato, considering the moral improvement of the people as the end of legislation, justly inferred that a law which commanded and threatened, but which neither convinced the reason nor touched the heart, must be a most imperfect law. He was not content with deterring from theft a man who still continued to be a thief at heart, with restraining a son who hated his mother from beating his mother. The only obedience on which he set much value was the obedience which an enlightened understanding yields to reason, and which a virtuous disposition yields to precepts of virtue. He really seems to have believed that, by prefixing to every law an eloquent and pathetic exhortation, he should, to a great extent, render penal enactments superfluous. Bacon entertained no such romantic hopes; and he well knew the practical inconveniences of the course which Plato recommended. "*Neque nobis*," says he, "*prologi legum qui inepti olim habiti sunt, et leges introducunt disputantes non jubentes, utique placerent, si priscos mores ferre possemus. . . . Quantum fieri potest prologi evitentur, et lex incipiat a jussione.*"

Each of the great men whom we have compared intended to illustrate his system by a philosophical romance; and each left his romance imperfect. Had Plato lived to finish the Critias, a comparison between that noble fiction and the New Atlantis would probably have furnished us with still more striking instances than any which we have given. It is amusing to think with what horror he would have seen such an institution as Solomon's House rising in his republic: with what vehemence he would have ordered the brewhouses, the perfume-houses, and the dispensatories to be pulled down; and with what inexorable rigour he would have driven beyond the frontier all the Fellows of the College, Merchants of Light and Depredators, Lamps and Pioneers.

To sum up the whole, we should say that the aim of the Platonic philosophy was to exalt man into a god. The aim of the Baconian philosophy was to provide man with what he requires while he continues to be man. The aim of the Platonic philosophy was to raise us far above vulgar wants. The aim of the Baconian philosophy was to supply our vulgar wants. The former aim was noble; but the latter was attainable. Plato drew a good bow: but, like Acestes in Virgil, he aimed at the stars; and therefore, though there was no want of strength or skill, the shot was thrown away. His arrow was indeed followed by a track of dazzling radiance, but it struck nothing.

"Volans liquidis in nubibus arsit arundo,
Signavitque viam flammis, tenuesque recessit
Consumta in ventos."

Bacon fixed his eye on a mark which was placed on the earth, and within bow-shot, and hit it in the white. The philosophy of Plato began in words and ended in words, noble words indeed, words such as were to be expected from the finest of human intellects exercising boundless dominion over the finest of human languages. The philosophy of Bacon began in observations and ended in arts.

The boast of the ancient philosophers was that their doctrine formed the minds of men to a high degree of wisdom and virtue. This was indeed the only practical good which the most celebrated of those teachers even pretended to effect; and undoubtedly, if they had effected this, they would have deserved far higher praise than if they had discovered the most salutary medicines or constructed the most powerful machines. But the truth is that, in those very matters in which alone they professed to do any good to mankind, in those very matters for the sake of which they neglected all the vulgar interests of mankind, they did nothing or worse than nothing. They promised what was impracticable; they despised what was practicable; they filled the world with long words and long beards; and they left it as wicked and as ignorant as they found it.

An acre in Middlesex is better than a principality in Utopia. The smallest actual good is better than the most magnificent promises of impossibilities. The wise man of the Stoics would, no doubt, be a grander object than a steam-engine. But there are steam-engines. And the wise man of the Stoics is yet to be born. A philosophy which should enable a man to feel perfectly happy while in agonies of pain would be better than a philosophy which assuages pain. But we know that there are remedies which will assuage pain; and we know that the ancient sages liked the toothache just as little as their neighbours. A philosophy which should extinguish cupidity would be better than a philosophy which should devise laws for the security of property. But it is possible to make laws which shall, to a very great extent, secure property. And we do not understand how any motives which the ancient philosophy furnished could extinguish cupidity. We know, indeed, that the philosophers were no better than other men. From the testimony of friends as well as of foes, from the confessions of Epictetus and Seneca, as well as from the sneers of Lucian and the fierce invectives of Juvenal, it is plain that these teachers of virtue had all the vices of their neighbours, with the additional vice of hypocrisy. Some people may think the object of the Baconian philosophy a low object, but they cannot deny that, high or low, it has been attained. They cannot deny that every year makes an addition to what Bacon called "fruit." They cannot deny that mankind have made, and are making, great and constant progress in the road which he pointed out to them.

Was there any such progressive movement among the ancient philosophers? After they had been declaiming eight hundred years, had they made the world better than when they began? Our belief is that, among the philosophers themselves, instead of a progressive improvement there was a progressive degeneracy. An abject superstition which Democritus or Anaxagoras would have rejected with scorn added the last disgrace to the long dotage of the Stoic and Platonic schools. Those unsuccessful attempts to articulate which are so delightful and interesting in a child, shock and disgust in an aged paralytic; and in the same way, those wild and mythological fictions which charm us, when we hear them lisped by Greek poetry in its infancy, excite a mixed sensation of pity and loathing when mumbled by Greek philosophy in its old age. We know that guns, cutlery, spy-glasses, clocks, are better in our time than they were in the time of our fathers, and were better in the time of our fathers than they were in the time of our grandfathers. We might, therefore, be inclined to think that, when a philosophy which boasted that its object was the elevation and purification of the mind, and which for this object neglected the sordid office of ministering to the comforts of the body, had flourished in the highest honour during many hundreds of years, a vast moral amelioration must have taken place. Was it so? Look at the schools of this wisdom four centuries before the Christian era and four centuries after that era. Compare the men whom those schools formed at those two periods. Compare Plato and Libanius. Compare Pericles and Julian. This philosophy confessed, nay boasted, that for every end but one it was useless. Had it attained that one end?

Suppose that Justinian, when he closed the schools of Athens, had called on the last few sages who still haunted the Portico, and lingered round the ancient plane-trees, to show their title to public veneration: suppose that he had said: "A thousand years have elapsed since, in this famous city, Socrates posed Protagoras and Hippias; during those thousand years a large proportion of the ablest men of every generation has been employed in constant efforts to bring to perfection the philosophy which you teach; that philosophy has been munificently patronised by the powerful; its professors have been held in the highest esteem by the public; it has drawn to itself almost all the sap and vigour of the human intellect: and what has it effected? What profitable truth has it taught us which we should not equally have known without it? What has it enabled us to do which we should not have been equally able to do without it?" Such questions, we suspect, would have puzzled Simplicius and Isidore. Ask a follower of Bacon what the new philosophy, as it was called in the time of Charles the Second, has effected for mankind, and his answer is ready: "It has lengthened life; it has mitigated pain; it has extinguished diseases; it has increased the fertility of the soil; it has given new securities to the mariner; it has furnished new arms to the warrior; it has spanned great rivers and estuaries with bridges of form unknown to our fathers; it has guided the thunderbolt innocuously from heaven to earth; it has lighted up the night with the splendour of the day; it has extended the range of the human vision; it has multiplied the power of the human muscles; it has accelerated motion; it has annihilated distance; it has facilitated intercourse, correspondence, all friendly offices, all despatch of business; it has enabled man to descend to the depths of the sea, to soar into the air, to penetrate securely into the noxious recesses of the earth, to traverse the land in cars which whirl along without horses, and the ocean in ships which run ten knots an hour against the wind. These are but a part of its fruits, and of its first fruits. For it is a philosophy which never rests, which has never attained, which is never perfect. Its law is progress. A point which yesterday was invisible is its goal to-day, and will be its starting-post to-morrow."

Great and various as the powers of Bacon were, he owes his wide and durable fame chiefly to this, that all those powers received their direction from common sense. His love of the vulgar useful, his strong sympathy with the popular notions of good and evil, and the openness with which he avowed that sympathy, are the secret of his influence. There was in his system no cant, no illusion. He had no anointing for broken bones, no fine theories *de finibus*, no arguments to persuade men out of their senses. He knew that men, and philosophers as well as other men, do actually love life, health, comfort, honour, security, the society of friends, and do actually dislike death, sickness, pain, poverty, disgrace, danger, separation from those to whom they are attached. He knew that religion, though it often regulates and moderates these feelings, seldom eradicates them; nor did he think it desirable for mankind that they should be eradicated. The plan of eradicating them by conceits like those of Seneca, or syllogisms like those of Chrysippus, was too preposterous to be for a moment entertained by a mind like his. He did not understand what wisdom there could be in changing names where it was impossible to change things; in denying that blindness, hunger, the gout, the rack, were evils, and calling them ἀποπροηγμένα: in refusing to acknowledge that health, safety, plenty, were good things, and dubbing them by the name of ἀδιάφορα. In his opinions on all these subjects, he was not a Stoic, nor an Epicurean, nor an Academic, but what would have been called by Stoics, Epicureans, and Academics a mere ἰδιώτης, a mere common man. And it was precisely because he was so that his name makes so great an era in the history of the world. It was because he dug deep that he was able to pile high. It was because, in order to lay his foundations, he went down into those parts of human nature which lie low, but which are not liable to change, that the fabric which he reared has risen to so stately an elevation, and stands with such immovable strength.

We have sometimes thought that an amusing fiction might be written, in which a disciple of Epictetus and a disciple of Bacon should be introduced as fellow-travellers. They come to a village where the small-pox has just begun to rage, and find houses shut up, intercourse suspended, the sick abandoned, mothers weeping in terror over their children. The Stoic assures the dismayed population that there is nothing bad in the small-pox, and that to a wise man disease, deformity, death, the loss of friends, are not evils. The Baconian takes out a lancet and begins to vaccinate. They find a body of miners in great dismay. An explosion of noisome vapours has just killed many of those who were at work; and the survivors are afraid to venture into the cavern. The Stoic assures them that such an accident is nothing but a mere ἀποπροηγμένον. The Baconian, who has no such fine word at his command, contents himself with devising a safety-lamp. They find a shipwrecked merchant wringing his hands on the shore. His vessel with an inestimable cargo has just gone down, and he is reduced in a moment from opulence to beggary. The Stoic exhorts him not to seek happiness in things which lie without himself, and repeats the whole chapter of Epictetus πρὸς τοὺς τὴν ἀπορίαν δεδοικότας. The Baconian constructs a diving-bell, goes down in it, and returns with the most precious effects from the wreck. It would be easy to multiply illustrations of the difference between the philosophy of thorns and the philosophy of fruit, the philosophy of words and the philosophy of works.

Bacon has been accused of overrating the importance of those sciences which minister to the physical well-being of man, and of underrating the importance of moral philosophy; and it cannot be denied that persons who read the *Novum Organum* and the *De Augmentis*, without adverting to the circumstances under which those works were written, will find much that may seem to countenance the accusation. It is certain, however, that, though in practice he often went very wrong, and though, as his historical work and his essays prove, he did not hold, even in theory, very strict opinions on points of political morality, he was far too wise a man not to know how much our well-being depends on the regulation of our minds. The world for which he wished was not, as some people seem to imagine, a world of water-wheels, power-looms, steam-carriages, sensualists, and knaves. He would have been as ready as Zeno himself to maintain that no bodily comforts which could be devised by the skill and labour of a hundred generations would give happiness to a man whose mind was under the tyranny of licentious appetite, of envy, of hatred, or of fear. If he sometimes appeared to ascribe importance too exclusively to the arts which increase the outward comforts of our species, the reason is plain. Those arts had been most unduly depreciated. They had been represented as unworthy of the attention of a man of liberal education. "*Cogitavit,*" says Bacon of himself, "*eam esse opinionem sive æstimationem humidam et damnosam, minui nempe majestatem mentis humanæ, si in experimentis et rebus particularibus, sensui subjectis, et in materia terminatis, diu ac multum versetur: præsertim cum hujusmodi res ad inquirendum laboriosæ, ad meditandum ignobiles, ad discendum asperæ, ad practicam illiberales, numero infinitæ, et subtilitate pusillæ videri soleant, et ob hujusmodi conditiones, gloriæ artium minus sint accommodatæ.*" This opinion seemed to him "*omnia in familia humana turbasse.*" It had undoubtedly caused many arts which were of the greatest utility, and which were susceptible of the greatest improvements, to be neglected by speculators, and abandoned to joiners, masons, smiths, weavers, apothecaries. It was necessary to assert the dignity of those arts, to bring them prominently forward, to proclaim that, as they have a most serious effect on human happiness, they are not unworthy of the attention of the highest human intellects. Again, it was by illustrations drawn from these arts that Bacon could most easily illustrate his principles. It was by improvements effected in these arts that the soundness of his principles could be most speedily and decisively brought to the test, and made manifest to common understandings. He acted like a wise commander who thins every other part of his line to strengthen a point where the enemy is attacking with peculiar fury, and on the fate of which the event of the battle seems likely to depend. In the *Novum Organum*, however, he distinctly and most truly declares that his philosophy is no less a moral than a Natural Philosophy, that, though his illustrations are drawn from physical science, the principles which those illustrations are intended to explain are just as applicable to ethical and political inquiries as to inquiries into the nature of heat and vegetation.

He frequently treated of moral subjects; and he brought to those subjects that spirit which was the essence of his whole system. He has left us many admirable practical observations on what he somewhat quaintly called the Georgics of the mind, on the mental culture which tends to produce good dispositions. Some persons, he said, might accuse him of spending labour on a matter so simple that his predecessors had passed it by with contempt. He desired such persons to remember that he had from the first announced the objects of his search to be not the splendid and the surprising, but the useful and the true, not the deluding dreams which go forth through the shining portal of ivory, but the humbler realities of the gate of horn.

True to this principle, he indulged in no rants about the fitness of things, the all-sufficiency of virtue, and the dignity of human nature. He dealt not at all in resounding nothings, such as those with which Bolingbroke pretended to comfort himself in exile, and in which Cicero vainly sought consolation after the loss of Tullia. The casuistical subtilties which occupied the attention of the keenest spirits of his age had, it should seem, no attractions for him. The doctors whom Escobar afterwards compared to the four beasts and the four-and-twenty elders in the Apocalypse Bacon dismissed with most contemptuous brevity. "*Inanes plerumque evadunt et futiles.*" Nor did he ever meddle with those enigmas which have puzzled hundreds of generations, and will puzzle hundreds more. He said nothing about the grounds of moral obligation, or the freedom of the human will. He had no inclination to employ himself in labours resembling those of the damned in the Grecian Tartarus, to spin for ever on the same wheel round the same pivot, to gape for ever after the same deluding clusters, to pour water for ever into the same bottomless buckets, to pace for ever to and fro on the same wearisome path after the same recoiling stone. He exhorted his disciples to prosecute researches of a very different description, to consider moral science as a practical science, a science of which the object was to cure the diseases and perturbations of the mind, and which could be improved only by a method analogous to that which has improved medicine and surgery. Moral philosophers ought, he said, to set themselves vigorously to work for the purpose of discovering what are the actual effects produced on the human character by particular modes of education, by the indulgence of particular habits, by the study of particular books, by society, by emulation, by imitation. Then we might hope to find out what mode of training was most likely to preserve and restore moral health.

What he was as a natural philosopher and a moral philosopher, that he was also as a theologian. He was, we are convinced, a sincere believer in the divine authority of the Christian revelation. Nothing can be found in his writings, or in any other writings, more eloquent and pathetic than some passages which were apparently written under the influence of strong devotional feeling. He loved to dwell on the power of the Christian religion to effect much that the ancient philosophers could only promise. He loved to consider that religion as the bond of charity, the curb of evil passions, the consolation of the wretched, the support of the timid, the hope of the dying. But controversies on speculative points of theology seem to have engaged scarcely any portion of his attention. In what he wrote on Church Government he showed, as far as he dared, a tolerant and charitable spirit. He troubled himself not at all about Homoousians and Homoiousians, Monothelites and Nestorians. He lived in an age in which disputes on the most subtle points of divinity excited an intense interest throughout Europe, and nowhere more than in England. He was placed in the very thick of the conflict. He was in power at the time of the Synod of Dort, and must for months have been daily deafened with talk about election, reprobation, and final perseverance. Yet we do not remember a line in his works from which it can be inferred that he was either a Calvinist or an Arminian. While the world was resounding with the noise of a disputatious philosophy and a disputatious theology, the Baconian school, like Alworthy seated between Square and Thwackum, preserved a calm neutrality, half scornful, half benevolent, and, content with adding to the sum of practical good, left the war of words to those who liked it.

We have dwelt long on the end of the Baconian philosophy, because from this peculiarity all the other peculiarities of that philosophy necessarily arose. Indeed, scarcely any person who proposed to himself the same end with Bacon could fail to hit upon the same means.

The vulgar notion about Bacon we take to be this,

that he invented a new method of arriving at truth, which method is called Induction, and that he detected some fallacy in the syllogistic reasoning which had been in vogue before his time. This notion is about as well-founded as that of the people who, in the middle ages, imagined that Virgil was a great conjurer. Many who are far too well-informed to talk such extravagant nonsense entertain what we think incorrect notions as to what Bacon really effected in this matter.

The inductive method has been practised ever since the beginning of the world by every human being. It is constantly practised by the most ignorant clown, by the most thoughtless schoolboy, by the very child at the breast. That method leads the clown to the conclusion that if he sows barley he shall not reap wheat. By that method the schoolboy learns that a cloudy day is the best for catching trout. The very infant, we imagine, is led by induction to expect milk from his mother or nurse, and none from his father.

Not only is it not true that Bacon invented the inductive method; but it is not true that he was the first person who correctly analysed that method and explained its uses. Aristotle had long before pointed out the absurdity of supposing that syllogistic reasoning could ever conduct men to the discovery of any new principle, had shown that such discoveries must be made by induction, and by induction alone, and had given the history of the inductive process, concisely indeed, but with great perspicuity and precision.

Again, we are not inclined to ascribe much practical value to that analysis of the inductive method which Bacon has given in the second book of the *Novum Organum*. It is indeed an elaborate and correct analysis. But it is an analysis of that which we are all doing from morning to night, and which we continue to do even in our dreams. A plain man finds his stomach out of order. He never heard Lord Bacon's name. But he proceeds in the strictest conformity with the rules laid down in the second book of the *Novum Organum*, and satisfies himself that mince pies have done the mischief. "I ate minced pies on Monday and Wednesday, and I was kept awake by indigestion all night." This is the *comparentia ad intellectum instantiarum convenientium*. "I did not eat any on Tuesday and Friday, and I was quite well." This is the *comparentia instantiarum in proximo quæ natura data privantur*. "I ate very sparingly of them on Sunday, and was very slightly indisposed in the evening. But on Christmas-day I almost dined on them, and was so ill that I was in great danger." This is the *comparentia instantiarum secundum magis et minus*. "It cannot have been the brandy which I took with them. For I have drunk brandy daily for years without being the worse for it." This is the *rejectio naturarum*. Our invalid then proceeds to what is termed by Bacon the

Vindemiatio, and pronounces that minced pies do not agree with him.

We repeat that we dispute neither the ingenuity nor the accuracy of the theory contained in the second book of the *Novum Organum;* but we think that Bacon greatly overrated its utility. We conceive that the inductive process, like many other processes, is not likely to be better performed merely because men know how they perform it. William Tell would not have been one whit more likely to cleave the apple if he had known that his arrow would describe a parabola under the influence of the attraction of the earth. Captain Barclay would not have been more likely to walk a thousand miles in a thousand hours if he had known the place and name of every muscle in his legs. Monsieur Jourdain probably did not pronounce D and F more correctly after he had been apprised that D is pronounced by touching the teeth with the end of the tongue, and F by putting the upper teeth on the lower lip. We cannot perceive that the study of Grammar makes the smallest difference in the speech of people who have always lived in good society. Not one Londoner in ten thousand can lay down the rules for the proper use of *will* and *shall.* Yet not one Londoner in a million ever misplaces his *will* and *shall.* Doctor Robertson could, undoubtedly, have written a luminous dissertation on the use of those words. Yet, even in his latest work, he sometimes misplaced them ludicrously. No man uses figures of speech with more propriety because he knows that one figure is called a metonymy and another a synecdoche. A drayman in a passion calls out, "You are a pretty fellow," without suspecting that he is uttering irony, and that irony is one of the four primary tropes. The old systems of rhetoric were never regarded by the most experienced and discerning judges as of any use for the purpose of forming an orator. "*Ego hanc vim intelligo*," said Cicero, "*esse in præceptis omnibus, non ut ea secuti oratores eloquentiæ laudem sint adepti, sed quæ sua sponte homines eloquentes facerent, ea quosdam observasse, atque id egisse; sic esse non eloquentiam ex artificio, sed artificium ex eloquentia natum.*" We must own that we entertain the same opinion concerning the study of Logic which Cicero entertained concerning the study of Rhetoric. A man of sense syllogises in *celarent* and *cesare* all day long without suspecting it; and, though he may not know what an *ignoratio elenchi* is, has no difficulty in exposing it whenever he falls in with it; which is likely to be as often as he falls in with a Reverend Master of Arts nourished on mode and figure in the cloisters of Oxford. Considered merely as an intellectual feat, the *Organum* of Aristotle can scarcely be admired too highly. But the more we compare individual with individual, school with school, nation with nation, generation with generation, the more do we lean to the opinion that the knowledge of the theory of logic has no tendency whatever to make men good reasoners.

What Aristotle did for the syllogistic process Bacon has, in the second book of the *Novum Organum*, done for the inductive process; that is to say, he has analysed it well. His rules are quite proper; but we do not need them, because they are drawn from our own constant practice.

But, though everybody is constantly performing the process described in the second book of the *Novum Organum*, some men perform it well, and some perform it ill. Some are led by it to truth, and some to error. It led Franklin to discover the nature of lightning. It led thousands, who had less brains than Franklin, to believe in animal magnetism. But this was not because Franklin went through the process described by Bacon, and the dupes of Mesmer through a different process. The *comparentiæ* and *rejectiones* of which we have given examples will be found in the most unsound inductions. We have heard that an eminent judge of the last generation was in the habit of jocosely propounding after dinner a theory, that the cause of the prevalence of Jacobinism was the practice of bearing three names. He quoted on the one side Charles James Fox, Richard Brinsley Sheridan, John Horne Tooke, John Philpot Curran, Samuel Taylor Coleridge, Theobald Wolfe Tone. These were *instantiæ convenientes*. He then proceeded to cite instances *absentiæ in proximo*, William Pitt, John Scott, William Windham, Samuel Horsley, Henry Dundas, Edmund Burke. He might have gone on to instances *secundum magis et minus*. The practice of giving children three names has been for some time a growing practice, and Jacobinism has also been growing. The practice of giving children three names is more common in America than in England. In England we still have a King and a House of Lords; but the Americans are republicans. The *rejectiones* are obvious. Burke and Theobald Wolfe Tone are both Irishmen; therefore the being an Irishman is not the cause of Jacobinism. Horsley and Horne Tooke are both clergymen; therefore the being a clergyman is not the cause of Jacobinism. Fox and Windham were both educated at Oxford; therefore the being educated at Oxford is not the cause of Jacobinism. Pitt and Horne Tooke were both educated at Cambridge; therefore the being educated at Cambridge is not the cause of Jacobinism. In this way, our inductive philosopher arrives at what Bacon calls the Vintage, and pronounces that the having three names is the cause of Jacobinism.

Here is an induction corresponding with Bacon's analysis, and ending in a monstrous absurdity. In what, then, does this induction differ from the induction which leads us to the conclusion that the presence of the sun is the cause of our having more light by day than by night? The difference evidently is not in the kind of instances, but in the number of instances; that is to say, the difference is not in that part of the process for which Bacon has given precise rules, but in a circumstance for which no precise rule can possibly be given. If the learned author of the theory about Jacobinism had enlarged either of his tables a little, his system would have been destroyed. The names of Tom Paine and William Wyndham Grenville would have been sufficient to do the work.

It appears to us, then, that the difference between a sound and unsound induction does not lie in this, that the author of the sound induction goes through the process analysed in the second book of the *Novum Organum*, and the author of the unsound induction through a different process. They both perform the same process. But one performs it foolishly or carelessly; the other performs it with patience, attention, sagacity, and judgment. Now precepts can do little towards making men patient and attentive, and still less towards making them sagacious and judicious. It is very well to tell men to be on their guard against prejudices, not to believe facts on slight evidence, not to be content with a scanty collection of facts, to put out of their minds the *idola* which Bacon has so finely described. But these rules are too general to be of much practical use. The question is, What is a prejudice? How long does the incredulity with which I hear a new theory propounded continue to be a wise and salutary incredulity?

When does it become an *idolum specus,* the unreasonable pertinacity of a too sceptical mind ? What is slight evidence ? What collection of facts is scanty ? Will ten instances do, or fifty, or a hundred ? In how many months would the first human beings who settled on the shores of the ocean have been justified in believing that the moon had an influence on the tides ? After how many experiments would Jenner have been justified in believing that he had discovered a safeguard against the small-pox ? These are questions to which it would be most desirable to have a precise answer; but, unhappily, they are questions to which no precise answer can be returned.

We think, then, that it is possible to lay down accurate rules, as Bacon has done, for the performing of that part of the inductive process which all men perform alike; but that these rules, though accurate, are not wanted, because in truth they only tell us to do what we are all doing. We think that it is impossible to lay down any precise rule for the performing of that part of the inductive process which a great experimental philosopher performs in one way, and a superstitious old woman in another.

On this subject, we think, Bacon was in an error. He certainly attributed to his rules a value which did not belong to them. He went so far as to say, that, if his method of making discoveries were adopted, little would depend on the degree of force or acuteness of any intellect; that all minds would be reduced to one level, that his philosophy resembled a compass or a rule which equalises all hands, and enables the most unpractised person to draw a more correct circle or line than the best draftsman can produce without such aid. This really seems to us as extravagant as it would have been in Lindley Murray to announce that everybody who should learn his grammar would write as good English as Dryden, or in that very able writer, the Archbishop of Dublin, to promise that all the readers of his Logic would reason like Chillingworth, and that all the readers of his Rhetoric would speak like Burke. That Bacon was altogether mistaken as to this point will now hardly be disputed. His philosophy has flourished during two hundred years, and has produced none of this levelling. The interval between a man of talents and a dunce is as wide as ever; and is never more clearly discernible than when they engage in researches which require the constant use of induction.

It will be seen that we do not consider Bacon's ingenious analysis of the inductive method as a very useful performance. Bacon was not, as we have already said, the inventor of the inductive method. He was not even the person who first analysed the inductive method correctly, though he undoubtedly analysed it more minutely than any who preceded him. He was not the person who first showed that by the inductive method alone new truth could be discovered. But he was the person who first turned the minds of speculative men, long occupied in verbal disputes, to the discovery of new and useful truth; and, by doing so, he at once gave to the inductive method an importance and dignity which had never before belonged to it. He was not the maker of that road; he was not the discoverer of that road; he was not the person who first surveyed and mapped that road. But he was the person who first called the public attention to an inexhaustible mine of wealth, which had been utterly neglected, and which was accessible by that road alone. By doing so he caused that road, which had previously been trodden only by peasants and higglers, to be frequented by a higher class of travellers.

That which was eminently his own in his system was the end which he proposed to himself. The end being given, the means, as it appears to us, could not well be mistaken. If others had aimed at the same object with Bacon, we hold it to be certain that they would have employed the same method with Bacon. It would have been hard to convince Seneca that the inventing of a safety-lamp was an employment worthy of a philosopher. It would have been hard to persuade Thomas Aquinas to descend from the making of syllogisms to the making of gunpowder. But Seneca would never have doubted for a moment that it was only by means of a series of experiments that a safety-lamp could be invented. Thomas Aquinas would never have thought that his *barbara* and *baralipton* would enable him to ascertain the proportion which charcoal ought to bear to saltpetre in a pound of gunpowder. Neither common sense nor Aristotle would have suffered him to fall into such an absurdity.

By stimulating men to the discovery of new truth, Bacon stimulated them to employ the inductive method, the only method, even the ancient philosophers and the schoolmen themselves being judges, by which new truth can be discovered. By stimulating men to the discovery of useful truth, he furnished them with a motive to perform the inductive process well and carefully. His predecessors had been, in his phrase, not interpreters, but anticipators of nature. They had been content with the first principles at which they had arrived by the most scanty and slovenly induction. And why was this? It was, we conceive, because their philosophy proposed to itself no practical end, because it was merely an exercise of the mind. A man who wants to contrive a new machine or a new medicine has a strong motive to observe accurately and patiently, and to try experiment after experiment. But a man who merely wants a theme for disputation or declamation has no such motive. He is therefore content with premises grounded on assumption, or on the most scanty and hasty induction. Thus, we conceive, the schoolmen acted. On their foolish premises they often argued with great ability; and as their object was "*assensum subjugare, non res,*" to be victorious in controversy, not to be victorious over nature, they were consistent. For just as much logical skill could be shown in reasoning on false as on true premises. But the followers of the new philosophy, proposing to themselves the discovery of useful truth as their object, must have altogether failed of attaining that object if they had been content to build theories on superficial induction.

Bacon has remarked that, in ages when philosophy was stationary, the mechanical arts went on improving. Why was this? Evidently because the mechanic was not content with so careless a mode of induction as served the purpose of the philosopher. And why was the philosopher more easily satisfied than the mechanic? Evidently because the object of the mechanic was to mould things, whilst the object of the philosopher was only to mould words. Careful induction is not at all necessary to the making of a good syllogism. But it is indispensable to the making of a good shoe. Mechanics, therefore, have always been, as far as the range of their humble but useful callings extended, not anticipators but interpreters of nature. And when a philosophy arose, the object of which was to do on a large scale what the mechanic does on a small scale, to extend the power and to supply the wants of man, the truth of the premises, which logically is a matter altogether unimportant, became a matter of the highest importance; and the careless induction with which men of learning had previously been satisfied, gave place, of necessity, to an induction far more accurate and satisfactory.

What Bacon did for inductive philosophy may, we think, be fairly stated thus. The objects of preceding speculators were objects which could be attained without careful induction. Those speculators, therefore, did not perform the inductive process carefully. Bacon stirred up men to pursue an object which could be attained only by induction, and by induction carefully performed; and consequently induction was more carefully performed. We do not think that the importance of what Bacon did for inductive philosophy has ever been overrated. But we think that the nature of his services is often mistaken, and was not fully understood even by himself. It was not by furnishing philosophers with rules for performing the inductive process well, but by furnishing them with a motive for performing it well, that he conferred so vast a benefit on society.

To give to the human mind a direction which it shall retain for ages is the rare prerogative of a few imperial spirits. It cannot, therefore, be uninteresting to inquire what was the moral and intellectual constitution which enabled Bacon to exercise so vast an influence on the world.

In the temper of Bacon—we speak of Bacon the philosopher, not of Bacon the lawyer and politician—

there was a singular union of audacity and sobriety. The promises which he made to mankind might, to a superficial reader, seem to resemble the rants which a great dramatist has put into the mouth of an Oriental conqueror half-crazed by good fortune and by violent passions.

> "He shall have chariots easier than air,
> Which I will have invented; and thyself
> That art the messenger shall ride before him,
> On a horse cut out of an entire diamond,
> That shall be made to go with golden wheels,
> I know not how yet."

But Bacon performed what he promised. In truth, Fletcher would not have dared to make Arbaces promise, in his wildest fits of excitement, the tithe of what the Baconian philosophy has performed.

The true philosophical temperament may, we think, be described in four words, much hope, little faith; a disposition to believe that anything, however extraordinary, may be done; an indisposition to believe that anything extraordinary has been done. In these points the constitution of Bacon's mind seems to us to have been absolutely perfect. He was at once the Mammon and the Surly of his friend Ben. Sir Epicure did not indulge in visions more magnificent and gigantic. Surly did not sift evidence with keener and more sagacious incredulity.

Closely connected with this peculiarity of Bacon's temper was a striking peculiarity of his understanding. With great minuteness of observation, he had an amplitude of comprehension such as has never yet been vouchsafed to any other human being. The small fine mind of Labruyère had not a more delicate tact than the large intellect of Bacon. The Essays contain abundant proofs that no nice feature of character, no peculiarity in the ordering of a house, a garden, or a court-masque, could escape the notice of one whose mind was capable of taking in the whole world of knowledge. His understanding resembled the tent which the fairy Paribanou gave to Prince Ahmed. Fold it; and it seemed a toy for the hand of a lady. Spread it; and the armies of powerful Sultans might repose beneath its shade.

In keenness of observation he has been equalled, though perhaps never surpassed. But the largeness of his mind was all his own. The glance with which he surveyed the intellectual universe resembled that which the Archangel, from the golden threshold of heaven, darted down into the new creation.

"Round he surveyed,—and well might, where he stood
So high above the circling canopy
Of night's extended shade,—from eastern point
Of Libra, to the fleecy star which bears
Andromeda far off Atlantic seas
Beyond the horizon."

His knowledge differed from that of other men, as a terrestrial globe differs from an Atlas which contains a different country on every leaf. The towns and roads of England, France, and Germany are better laid down in the Atlas than on the globe. But while we are looking at England we see nothing of France; and while we are looking at France we see nothing of Germany. We may go to the Atlas to learn the bearings and distances of York and Bristol, or of Dresden and Prague. But it is useless if we want to know the bearings and distances of France and Martinique, or of England and Canada. On the globe we shall not find all the market towns in our own neighbourhood; but we shall learn from it the comparative extent and the relative position of all the kingdoms of the earth. "I have taken," said Bacon, in a letter written when he was only thirty-one, to his uncle, Lord Burleigh, "I have taken all knowledge to be my province." In any other young man, indeed in any other man, this would have been a ridiculous flight of presumption. There have been thousands of better mathematicians, astronomers, chemists, physicians, botanists, mineralogists, than Bacon. No man would go to Bacon's works to learn any particular science or art, any more than he would go to a twelve-inch globe in order to find his way from Kennington turnpike to Clapham Common. The art which Bacon taught was the art of inventing arts. The knowledge in which Bacon excelled all men was a knowledge of the mutual relations of all departments of knowledge.

The mode in which he communicated his thoughts was peculiar to him. He had no touch of that disputatious temper which he often censured in his predecessors. He effected a vast intellectual revolution in opposition to a vast mass of prejudices; yet he never engaged in any controversy: nay, we cannot at present recollect, in all his philosophical works, a single passage of a controversial character. All those works might with propriety have been put into the form which he adopted in the work entitled *Cogitata et visa:* " *Franciscus Baconus sic cogitavit.*" These are thoughts which have occurred to me: weigh them well, and take them or leave them.

Borgia said of the famous expedition of Charles the Eighth, that the French had conquered Italy, not with steel, but with chalk; for that the only exploit which they had found necessary for the purpose of taking military occupation of any place had been to mark the doors of the houses where they meant to quarter. Bacon often quoted this saying, and loved to apply it to the victories of his own intellect. His philosophy, he said, came as a guest, not as an enemy. She found no difficulty in gaining admittance, without a contest, into every understanding fitted, by its structure and by its capacity, to receive her. In all this we think that he acted most judiciously; first, because, as he has himself remarked, the difference between his school and other schools was a difference so fundamental that there was hardly any common ground on which a controversial battle could be fought; and secondly, because his mind, eminently observant, pre-eminently discursive and capacious, was, we conceive, neither formed by nature nor disciplined by habit for dialectical combat.

Though Bacon did not arm his philosophy with the weapons of logic, he adorned her profusely with all the richest decorations of rhetoric. His eloquence, though not untainted with the vicious taste of his age, would alone have entitled him to a high rank in literature. He had a wonderful talent for packing thought close, and rendering it portable. In wit, if by wit be meant the power of perceiving analogies between things which appear to have nothing in common, he never had an equal, not even Cowley, not even the author of Hudibras. Indeed, he possessed this faculty, or rather this faculty possessed him, to a morbid degree. When he abandoned himself to it without reserve, as he did in the *Sapientia Veterum*, and at the end of the second book of the *De Augmentis*, the feats which he performed were not merely admirable, but portentous, and almost shocking. On those occasions we marvel at him as clowns on a fair-day marvel at a juggler, and can hardly help thinking that the devil must be in him.

These, however, were freaks in which his ingenuity now and then wantoned, with scarcely any other object than to astonish and amuse. But it occasionally happened that, when he was engaged in grave and profound investigations, his wit obtained the mastery over all his other faculties, and led him into absurdities into which no dull man could possibly have fallen. We will give the most striking instance which at present occurs to us. In the third book of the *De Augmentis* he tells us that there are some principles which are not peculiar to one science, but are common to several. That part of philosophy which concerns itself with these principles is, in his nomenclature, designated as *philosophia prima*. He then proceeds to mention some of the principles with which this *philosophia prima* is conversant. One of them is this. An infectious disease is more likely to be communicated while it is in progress than when it has reached its height. This, says he, is true in medicine. It is also true in morals; for we see that the example of very abandoned men injures public morality less than the example of men in whom vice has not yet extinguished all good qualities. Again, he tells us that in music a discord ending in a concord is agreeable, and that the same thing may be noted in the affections. Once more, he tells us that in physics the energy with which a principle acts is often increased by the antiperistasis of its opposite; and that it is the same in the contests of factions. If the making of ingenious and sparkling similitudes like these be indeed the *philosophia prima*, we are quite sure that the greatest philosophical work of the nineteenth century is Mr. Moore's Lalla Rookh. The similitudes which we have cited are very happy similitudes. But that a man like Bacon should have taken them for more, that he should have thought the discovery of such resemblances as these an important part of philosophy, has always appeared to us one of the most singular facts in the history of letters.

The truth is that his mind was wonderfully quick in perceiving analogies of all sorts. But, like several eminent men whom we could name, both living and dead, he sometimes appeared strangely deficient in the power of distinguishing rational from fanciful analogies, analogies which are arguments from analogies which are mere illustrations, analogies like that which Bishop Butler so ably pointed out, between natural and revealed religion, from analogies like that which Addison discovered, between the series of Grecian gods carved by Phidias and the series of English kings painted by Kneller. This want of discrimination has led to many strange political speculations. Sir William Temple deduced a theory of government from the properties of the pyramid. Mr. Southey's whole system of finance is grounded on the phenomena of evaporation and rain. In theology, this perverted ingenuity has made still wilder work. From the time of Irenæus and Origen down to the present day, there has not been a single generation in which great divines have not been led into the most absurd expositions of Scripture, by mere incapacity to distinguish analogies proper, to use the scholastic phrase, from analogies metaphorical. It is curious that Bacon has himself mentioned this very kind of delusion among the *idola specus*; and has mentioned it in language which, we are inclined to think, shows that he knew himself to be subject to it. It is the vice, he tells us, of subtle minds to attach too much importance to slight distinctions; it is the vice, on the other hand, of high and discursive intellects to attach too much importance to slight resemblances; and he adds that, when this last propensity is indulged to excess, it leads men to catch at shadows instead of substances.

Yet we cannot wish that Bacon's wit had been less luxuriant. For, to say nothing of the pleasure which it affords, it was in the vast majority of cases employed for the purpose of making obscure truth plain, of making repulsive truth attractive, of fixing in the mind for ever truth which might otherwise have left but a transient impression.

The poetical faculty was powerful in Bacon's mind, but not, like his wit, so powerful as occasionally to usurp the place of his reason, and to tyrannise over the whole man. No imagination was ever at once so strong and so thoroughly subjugated. It never stirred but at a signal from good sense. It stopped at the first check from good sense. Yet, though disciplined to such obedience, it gave noble proofs of its vigour. In truth, much of Bacon's life was passed in a visionary world, amidst things as strange as any that are described in the Arabian Tales, or in those romances on which the curate and barber of Don Quixote's village performed so cruel an *auto da fe*, amidst buildings more sumptuous than the palace of Aladdin, fountains more wonderful than the golden water of Parizade, conveyances more rapid than the hippogryph of Ruggiero, arms more formidable than the lance of Astolfo, remedies more efficacious than the balsam of Fierabras. Yet in his magnificent day-dreams there was nothing wild, nothing but what sober reason sanctioned. He knew that all the secrets feigned by poets to have been written in the books of enchanters are worthless when compared with the mighty secrets which are really written in the book of nature, and which, with time and patience, will be read there. He knew that all the wonders wrought by all the talismans in fable were trifles when compared to the wonders which might reasonably be expected from the philosophy of fruit, and that, if his words sank deep into the minds of men, they would produce effects such as superstition had never ascribed to the incantations of Merlin and Michael Scott. It was here that he loved to let his imagination loose. He loved to picture to himself the world as it would be when his philosophy should, in his own noble phrase, "have enlarged the bounds of human empire." We might refer to many instances. But we will content ourselves with the strongest, the description of the House of Solomon in the New Atlantis. By most of Bacon's contemporaries, and by some people of our time, this remarkable passage would, we doubt not, be considered as an ingenious rodomontade, a counterpart to the adventures of Sindbad or Baron Munchausen. The truth is that there is not to be found in any human composition a passage more eminently distinguished by profound and serene wisdom. The boldness and originality of the fiction is far less wonderful than the nice discernment which carefully excluded from that long list of prodigies everything that can be pronounced impossible, everything that can be proved to lie beyond the mighty magic of induction and of time. Already some parts, and not the least startling parts, of this glorious prophecy have been accomplished, even according to the letter; and the whole, construed according to the spirit, is daily accomplishing all around us.

One of the most remarkable circumstances in the history of Bacon's mind is the order in which its powers expanded themselves. With him the fruit came first and remained till the last; the blossoms did not appear till late. In general, the development of the fancy is to the development of the judgment what the growth of a girl is to the growth of a boy. The fancy attains at an earlier period to the perfection of its beauty, its power, and its fruitfulness; and, as it is first to ripen, it is also first to fade. It has generally lost something of its bloom and freshness before the sterner faculties have reached maturity; and is commonly withered and barren while those faculties still retain all their energy. It rarely happens that the fancy and the judgment grow together. It happens still more rarely that the judgment grows faster than the fancy. This seems, however, to have been the case with Bacon. His boyhood and youth appear to have been singularly sedate. His gigantic scheme of philosophical reform is said by some writers to have been planned before he was fifteen, and was undoubtedly planned while he was still young. He observed as vigilantly, meditated as deeply, and judged as temperately when he gave his first work to the world as at the close of his long career. But in eloquence, in sweetness and variety of expression, and in richness of illustration, his later writings are far superior to those of his youth. In this respect the history of his mind bears some resemblance to the history of the mind of Burke. The treatise on the Sublime and Beautiful, though written on a subject which the coldest metaphysician could hardly treat without being occasionally betrayed into florid writing, is the most unadorned of all Burke's works. It appeared when he was twenty-five or twenty-six. When, at forty, he wrote the Thoughts on the Causes of the existing Discontents, his reason and his judgment had reached their full maturity; but his eloquence was still in its splendid dawn. At fifty, his rhetoric was quite as rich as good taste would permit; and when he died, at almost seventy, it had become ungracefully gorgeous. In his youth he wrote on the emotions produced by mountains and cascades, by the masterpieces of painting and sculpture, by the faces and necks of beautiful women, in the style of a parliamentary report. In his old age he discussed treaties and tariffs in the most fervid and brilliant language of romance. It is strange that the Essay on the Sublime and Beautiful, and the Letter to a Noble Lord, should be the productions of one man. But it is far more strange that the Essay should have been a production of his youth, and the Letter of his old age.

We will give very short specimens of Bacon's two styles. In 1597 he wrote thus: "Crafty men contemn studies; simple men admire them; and wise men use them; for they teach not their own use: that is a wisdom without them, and won by observation. Read not to contradict, nor to believe, but to weigh and consider. Some books are to be tasted, others to be swallowed, and some few to be chewed and digested. Reading maketh a full man, conference a ready man, and writing an exact man. And therefore if a man write little, he had need have a great memory; if he confer little, have a present wit: and if he read little, have much cunning to seem to know that he doth not. Histories make men wise, poets witty, the mathematics subtle, natural philosophy deep, morals grave, logic and rhetoric able to contend." It will hardly be disputed that this is a passage to be "chewed and digested." We do not believe that Thucydides himself has anywhere compressed so much thought into so small a space.

In the additions which Bacon afterwards made to the Essays, there is nothing superior in truth or weight to what we have quoted. But his style was constantly becoming richer and softer. The following passage, first published in 1625, will show the extent of the change: "Prosperity is the blessing of the Old Testament; adversity is the blessing of the New, which carrieth the greater benediction and the clearer evidence of God's favour. Yet, even in the Old Testament, if you listen to David's harp you shall hear as many hearse-like airs as carols; and the pencil of the Holy Ghost hath laboured more in describing the afflictions of Job than the felicities of Solomon. Prosperity is not without many fears and distastes; and adversity is not without comforts and hopes. We see in needle-works and embroideries it is more pleasing to have a lively work upon a sad and solemn ground, than to have a dark and melancholy work upon a lightsome ground. Judge therefore of the pleasure of the heart by the pleasure of the eye. Certainly virtue is like precious odours, most fragrant when they are incensed or crushed; for prosperity doth best discover vice, but adversity doth best discover virtue."

It is by the Essays that Bacon is best known to the multitude. The *Novum Organum* and the *De Augmentis* are much talked of, but little read. They have produced, indeed, a vast effect on the opinions of mankind; but they have produced it through the operation of intermediate agents. They have moved the intellects which have moved the world. It is in the Essays alone that the mind of Bacon is brought into immediate contact with the minds of ordinary readers. There he opens an exoteric school and talks to plain men, in language which everybody understands, about things in which everybody is interested. He has thus enabled those who must otherwise have taken his merits on trust to judge for themselves; and the great body of readers have, during several generations, acknowledged that the man who has treated with such consummate ability questions with which they are familiar may well be supposed to deserve all the praise bestowed on him by those who have sat in his inner school.

Without any disparagement to the admirable treatise

De Augmentis, we must say that, in our judgment, Bacon's greatest performance is the first book of the *Novum Organum*. All the peculiarities of his extraordinary mind are found there in the highest perfection. Many of the aphorisms, but particularly those in which he gives examples of the influence of the *idola*, show a nicety of observation that has never been surpassed. Every part of the book blazes with wit, but with wit which is employed only to illustrate and decorate truth. No book ever made so great a revolution in the mode of thinking, overthrew so many prejudices, introduced so many new opinions. Yet no book was ever written in a less contentious spirit. It truly conquers with chalk and not with steel. Proposition after proposition enters into the mind, is received not as an invader, but as a welcome friend, and, though previously unknown, becomes at once domesticated. But what we most admire is the vast capacity of that intellect which, without effort, takes in at once all the domains of science, all the past, the present, and the future, all the errors of two thousand years, all the encouraging signs of the passing times, all the bright hopes of the coming age. Cowley, who was among the most ardent, and not among the least discerning followers of the new philosophy, has, in one of his finest poems, compared Bacon to Moses standing on Mount Pisgah. It is to Bacon, we think, as he appears in the first book of the

Novum Organum, that the comparison applies with peculiar felicity. There we see the great Law-giver looking round from his lonely elevation on an infinite expanse; behind him a wilderness of dreary sands and bitter waters, in which successive generations have sojourned, always moving, yet never advancing, reaping no harvest, and building no abiding city; before him a goodly land, a land of promise, a land flowing with milk and honey. While the multitude below saw only the flat sterile desert in which they had so long wandered, bounded on every side by a near horizon, or diversified only by some deceitful mirage, he was gazing from a far higher stand on a far lovelier country, following with his eye the long course of fertilising rivers, through ample pastures, and under the bridges of great capitals, measuring the distances of marts and havens, and portioning out all those wealthy regions from Dan to Beersheba.

It is painful to turn back from contemplating Bacon's philosophy to contemplate his life. Yet without so turning back it is impossible fairly to estimate his powers. He left the University at an earlier age than that at which most people repair thither. While yet a boy he was plunged into the midst of diplomatic business. Thence he passed to the study of a vast technical system of law, and worked his way up through a succession of laborious offices to the highest post in his profession. In the meantime he took an active part in every Parliament; he was an adviser of the Crown; he paid court with the greatest assiduity and address to all whose favour was likely to be of use to him; he lived much in society; he noted the slightest peculiarities of character and the slightest changes of fashion. Scarcely any man has led a more stirring life than that which Bacon led from sixteen to sixty. Scarcely any man has been better entitled to be called a thorough man of the world. The founding of a new philosophy, the imparting of a new direction to the minds of speculators, this was the amusement of his leisure, the work of hours occasionally stolen from the Woolsack and the Council Board. This consideration, while it increases the admiration with which we regard his intellect, increases also our regret that such an intellect should so often have been unworthily employed. He well knew the better course, and had, at one time, resolved to pursue it. "I confess," said he, in a letter written when he was still young, "that I have as vast contemplative ends as I have moderate civil ends." Had his civil ends continued to be moderate, he would have been, not only the Moses, but the Joshua of philosophy. He would have fulfilled a large part of his own magnificent predictions. He would have led his followers, not only to the verge, but into the heart of the promised land. He would not merely have pointed out, but would have divided the spoil. Above all, he would have left, not only a great, but a spotless name. Mankind would then have been able to esteem their illustrious benefactor. We should not then be compelled to regard his character with mingled contempt and admiration, with mingled aversion and gratitude. We should not then regret that there should be so many proofs of the narrowness and selfishness of a heart, the benevolence of which was yet large enough to take in all races and all ages. We should not then have to blush for the disingenuousness of the most devoted worshipper of speculative truth, for the servility of the boldest champion of intellectual freedom. We should not then have seen the same man at one time far in the van, and at another time far in the rear of his generation. We should not then be forced to own that he who first treated legislation as a science was among the last Englishmen who used the rack, that he who first summoned philosophers to the great work of interpreting nature was among the last Englishmen who sold justice. And we should conclude our survey of a life placidly, honourably, beneficently passed, "in industrious observations, grounded conclusions, and profitable inventions and discoveries," with feelings very different from those with which we now turn away from the checkered spectacle of so much glory and so much shame.

THE END.

www.ingramcontent.com/pod-product-compliance
Lightning Source LLC
Chambersburg PA
CBHW011341090426
42743CB00018B/3412